Shakespeare's Spiritual Sonnets

John T. Noonan Jr

ISBN-10: 1456586831

EAN-13: 9781456586836

Library of Congress Control Number: 2011901658

CreateSpace, North Charleston, South Carolina

But the vanity of man cannot counterpoyse the authority of God, who . . . by his Apostle willing us to exercise our devotion in Himnes and Spiritual Sonnets, waranteth the Art to be good and the use allowable.

St. Robert Southwell

To the memory

of

my tutors in the tradition,

Walter Jackson Bate

and

Harry Levin

Table of Contents

Acknowledgments

I am indebted above all to the advice, encouragement, and sustaining love of my wife, Mary Lee, and to the enthusiasm of my three children, John, Becky and Susie, for my project. Without assigning any responsibility for my claims or for my errors, I thank those who have read the manuscript: the late Thomas G. Barnes, Professor of History and Law, emeritus, University of California, Berkeley; Reverend Owen Carroll, Professor of Theology, Dominican School of Theology, and Professor of Philosophy, St. Mary's College; Dagfinn Føllesdal, Clarence Irving Lewis Professor of Philosophy, Stanford University; Vera Føllesdal, critic's critic and truthful translator; Joseph Kerman, Professor of Music, emeritus, University of California, Berkeley; my sister Marie Sabin, scholar of Scripture; James Sheehan, Dickason Professor in the Humanities and Professor of Modern European History, Stanford University, and past President of the American Historical Association; and Joseph Vining, Harry Burns Hutchins Professor of Law, University of Michigan Law School. I thank John Maguire for his helpful interest. I thank Joseph Gratz, astute assistant. I appreciate the research of Susan Willoughby Anderson, Julian Park, Suzanne Stolezenberg and Trevor Wedman. I have a particular debt to the patient decoding of my handwriting by Evelyn Lew in order to produce many drafts and a final manuscript. I thank for their prompt and helpful responses to specific inquiries: John W. O'Malley, S.J., Scott Pilarz, S.J., and Norman Tanner, S.J. I am further indebted to Peter Milward, S.J. for the gift of his *Shakespeare's Religious Background*

(1973) and to Thomas M. McCoog, S.J. for the gift of his *The Reckoned Expense. Edmund Campion and the Early English Jesuits* (2nd ed., 2007) – two books, whose scholarship and disagreement display a healthy and remarkable range of judgments within a single religious order. I am equally indebted to Peter Davidson for the gift of *St. Robert Southwell, S.J.: Collected Poems*, edited by Davidson and Anne Sweeney. Harry Cronin, C.S.C. directed my attention to the Shakespeare allusion in Eugene O'Neill and to further exploration of Southwell. I owe a debt difficult to define to the Ashland Shakespeare Festival, whose plays and players have for twenty-four years stimulated and challenged my sense of the spirit of Shakespeare. I thank the Huntington Library for permitting me to examine its copy of *Loves Martyr* (1601), one of three copies extant. Of the thirteen existing examples of the original edition of the Sonnets in 1609, the Huntington holds two. I deeply appreciate its courtesy in permitting an examination of these copies by Mary Lee and me.

John T. Noonan, Jr.

December 8, 2010
Berkeley, California

1. The Argument of This Book

In an age marked by martyrdom, William Shakespeare, supreme of poets, wrote spiritual poetry of matchless beauty and intensity. This volume incorporates that poetry. The principal exhibits are the selected sonnets that I shall style the Spiritual Sonnets or the Twenty-two, supplemented by what I shall call the *Loves Martyr* poem. In my interpretation, I depart radically from the conventional readings.

On three points I am in agreement with conventional interpretation:

1. The Twenty-two reflect the experience and convictions of the poet.

2. Many of them are expressly autobiographical.

3. Many of them are poems of love.

On four points, I disagree with the traditional readings and believe the following:

1. The Twenty-two cannot be read as part of two or three sustained narratives.

2. The Twenty-two all have specific addressees.

3. It is important to discover who these addressees are.

4. The love expressed is not always the love of one human being for another human being now on earth.

The sense of the Spiritual Sonnets cannot be garnered simply from a close inspection of texts or by an elucidation of their vocabulary and word play or by an imaginative reconstruction of the sex life of

Shakespeare. The Twenty-two must be read in context. That context is, first, provided by the several communities in which Shakespeare lived. Most pertinent here is a fragmented community shaped by the unevenly applied Elizabethan statutes governing religious authority, religious controversy, religious missionaries, and religious worship. Within the fragmented community, William Byrd and Robert Southwell offer clues to Shakespeare. Byrd demonstrates how a master of his art could work to enhearten his disfavored community at the same time that he preserved his place in the Elizabethan establishment. Southwell, who was sought and caught as a priest criminally present in England, provides images and insights that Shakespeare adapted in his plays. He also gave advice on the writing of sonnets that may be read as advice the playwright took.

The chapter on this community sets the stage. The second chapter brings together the bits of biographical information that patient scholars have assembled bearing on the poet's religious beliefs – what was said about him when he was alive and what is known of his family, his schoolteachers, his schoolmates, and his patrons. What I set out is not new; it is relevant. Inconclusive as the data are, they are supplemented by what may be gleaned from the plays, but not from individual lines given to the characters to express their own beliefs and emotions. Tantalizing allusions, unnecessary to a play's plot, occur – for example, to Mary, Queen of Scots, and to Edmund Campion, S.J., each of whom was revered as a martyr by Shakespeare's Catholic contemporaries. As Stephen Greenblatt has demonstrated, a Catholic preoccupation with purgatory has a central role in *Hamlet*. The whole structure of *Measure for Measure* turns on the redemptive grace of an act of forgiveness.

The great plays throb with themes that only a deeply religious consciousness would explore. Study of English in my college days identified Shakespeare's religious consciousness with the Elizabethan Church or, alternatively, with the despair of *Lear*; or again, it was hailed in Matthew Arnold's verse as beyond any mortal's guess. Today Arnold's agnosticism is still popular. Others hold that the author of *Lear* had no beliefs. A global icon, Shakespeare is not to be confined to any creed. A few, like Gary Taylor, argue that whatever he believed is irrelevant. When a few years ago, I read that Shakespeare had been mixed up with Jesuits, I was as ready to believe it as if I had read that he was actually under Communist Party discipline. Jesuits, the Counter-Reformation Church, and canonized saints of that Church had never entered into my mind in studying Shakespeare. Taking into account this new information, rereading the plays, I argue that irreligion is an attribution to Shakespeare that is false and that the irrelevancy of his religion is equally so. It's worth an effort to discover more.

The poem which Shakespeare contributed in 1601 to the collection entitled *Loves Martyr* affords opportunity for such an effort, the subject of chapter three. In the form of an allegory about birds, the poem is a requiem for a young woman hung at Tyburn, February 27, 1601. The poet has disregarded the purpose of his patron and chosen to compose an exquisite lament for Anne Line, tried for harboring a priest, convicted, and executed. The poem is decisive proof of Shakespeare's knowledge of the Catholic community as it existed in London. If he knew it well and risked writing about its martyrs, it seems plausible that he shared its beliefs. His celebration of the dead criminal, put in Aesopian allegory, is testimony to his thought in his maturity.

The London context as well as the Stratford context, are settings in which the Sonnets are to be understood. The contexts need to be enlarged to include the continent. Shakespeare was not an island. He was part of the main. He was a participant in the culture of contemporary Europe where his plays are so often set. He was deep in its tradition that had been fashioned over one thousand years. Its religious roots, its cultural heritage, its currents of theology need to be taken into account. The poet of the Sonnets is a man of his time and of his place. His place is not merely provincial, not merely insular. If he is the man of the millennium, as he has recently been called, it is a millennium that began with Gregory the Great's dispatch of missionaries to unenlightened Britain.

Tentatively, then more confidently, always aware of difficulties, I came to understand twenty-two of the one hundred and fifty-four Sonnets as having addressees (or in one case, a speaker) whose identity it is important to determine. Chapter Four sets out the arguments. Chapters Five through Eleven focus on particular sonnets. Chapter Twelve recapitulates and concludes.

Two of the sonnets are in a medieval mode: a discourse with the poet's own soul; their spiritual content is on their surface and at their heart; scriptural language evokes scriptural judgments. Three of the sonnets address the modern missionaries, the English Jesuits dispatched from Rome to reclaim England for the old faith. The collectivity addressed is no single person. One sonnet has an unusual speaker: the old, the battered, the almost extinguished Church, nourished nonetheless by the death of her martyrs. In twelve sonnets, the poet addresses Mother Church herself, acknowledging his faults, praying for mercy, vowing repentance. In two sonnets, the Virgin Mother replaces the Church as the repository of his pleas and hopes. Two sonnets are spoken directly to God, one addressing the author of natural law; the other, God in the Eucharist.

How do I reach my conclusions so likely to strike a casual reader as antecedently impossible? I have approached the Shakespeare of the Twenty-two as the man hinted at by the biographical bits; the man reflected in isolated lines or in structural themes in the plays; the close reader of Southwell; the composer of Anne Line's requiem. But my exegesis of the Twenty-two has required the examination of each of them to establish addressee and meaning by evidence internal to each poem, evidence then interpreted to prove the case.

Part of that proof is negative. It consists in showing that the conventional interpretations strain credibility, distort individual lines, overlook whole quatrains, and occasionally produce sheer unintelligibility. Proof positive consists in lines, in quatrains, in concluding couplets, in complete sonnets that rime the sins and repentance, the supplications and aspirations, the hopes and the self-offering of their creator. So read, the Twenty-two ring the chords of the heart.

Euclidean logic concluding with a Q.E.D. cannot be used in matters of literature. Proof is by probabilities – one probability interacting with another, one interpretation interlocking with another until persuasive coherence is achieved and with it the conviction that the Spiritual Sonnets are the spiritual testament of William Shakespeare.

Read the Twenty-two afresh. See them as newly minted. Hear with your heart.

2. Precarious Community

The community in which to consider Shakespeare and his spiritual poetry was shaped by the law regarding religion in England. That law had changed dramatically in the sixteenth century, taking England from a country in which the Catholic Church shared governmental power with the Crown to one in which the monarch was the lawful head of the Church and those who adhered to the old, papally-administered Church were not obedient to the law and, if not careful, risked being treated as criminals and even as traitors.

The Law. The substantial shift in the legal status of certain religious beliefs was effected by the holders of authority beginning with Henry VIII and carried out with varying degrees of conviction throughout a nation that did respond, however idiosyncratically, to royal direction. *Duffy* 1992 570-573. As modern historians have now demonstrated, the changes came largely from above, were not the product of popular enthusiasm, and were very hard for some to swallow. Caught between the pressures of the law and traditional ways of thought, perplexed by the conflicting demands of patriotism and fidelity to an older way, many preferred to avoid costly commitments, to see but not judge, to accommodate as much as possible. For example, a close study of wills probated in Gloucestershire from 1540 to 1580 shows a sharp decline in traditional Catholic preambles, a small and steady number of Protestant preambles, and a steep rise in ambiguous preambles. *Lutzenberger* 174. As the religious lines were drawn by Henry VIII and redrawn by Edward VI and by Mary and by Elizabeth and by James, the size of the change in religion became clear. Some still preferred not to acknowledge that the past was irretrievable.

The first English martyr unreconciled to the new establishment was John Hougton, educated as a lawyer at Cambridge, a Carthusian, prior of the London Charterhouse. *Caraman*, "Martyrs" 325. His death in 1533 was followed by that of two men of even higher rank, John Fisher, bishop of Rochester, made a cardinal while imprisoned; and Henry VIII's ex-chancellor and ex-friend, Thomas More. Martyrs continued to be made under Elizabeth. John Donne could not keep from noticing sun-parched quarters on the city gate.

Donne, *Satires* II.31.

The torture and the killing of contemporaries, of persons one knew, of friends, of relatives had an immediacy that no reading of ancient martyrdoms or the Acts of the Apostles with its account of the first martyr, Stephen, could supply. The deaths inflicted were hideous. Only faith could see them as triumphs:

> His quarters hung on every gate does show
> His doctrine sound through countries far and near
> His head set up so high doth call for more
> To fight the fight which he endured here.

Gregory 283, quoting "A Dialogue between a Catholic, and Consolation."

The law, as it evolved under Elizabeth, was simple, comprehensive and increasingly responsive to what the government saw as the threat from the Catholicism that had been banned. The first legislation enacted under Elizabeth in 1559 consisted in an act restoring to the Queen "jurisdiction over the state, ecclesiastical and spiritual, and abolishing all foreign power repugnant to the same." 1 Eliz. c.1. The ecclesiastical legislation of Philip and Mary was repealed, that of Henry VIII and Edward VI restored, and the Queen was described as "the only supreme governor of this realm in all spiritual or temporal things." Every holder of ecclesiastical office was to acknowledge her position by an oath and, failing so to swear, was to be deprived of office. Every defender of foreign jurisdiction was for his first offense to lose all his property, and for his third, to suffer death and other penalties as in the case of high treason. A companion piece of legislation was an act "for the uniformity of common prayer." Anyone speaking out against the *Book of Common Prayer* was, for the third offense, subject to life imprisonment. Any person not attending divine service on Sundays was subject to a fine of 12 pence, to be levied by the churchwardens and enforced by the bishops and by the justices of the peace. 1 Eliz. c.2.

The "romish religion" was described as heresy, but heresy as such was not punished. The two statutes punished what was palpable, not belief, only conduct and speech. Good lawyers, the legislative draftsmen saw that jurisdiction was the key. Who could deny the Queen jurisdiction in her own realm? On this foundation, the Church of England was established and the Church of Rome banished from the land.

The Church of England was secure unless it was undermined from abroad; the priests still alive in England, ordained under Henry VIII or Mary, could be expected to die off quietly. Attack from abroad came. In 1570, Pius V excommunicated Elizabeth, in Rome's view thereby relieving her subjects of obligation to obey her. In 1571, new English legislation, 13 Eliz. c.1, identified as high treason any word or speech denying the queen's authority. A companion chapter specifically legislated against "bringing in and putting in execution" bulls and other instruments from Rome, actions also marked as high treason. Young Englishmen were leaving their island and going to seminaries on the continent, particularly Douai, where they were trained as priests. A third statute of 1571, 13 Eliz. c.3, noted this phenomenon, and, observing that persons "do secretly and in great numbers" depart the realm, required "the fugitives'" to return in six months and permitted no further departures except by express license of the queen; penalty, the loss of all income from one's lands.

In the story of foreign aggression told by the English government the Jesuits held a special place. With Pope Paul III's approval in 1540 of their basic formula of organization, the Society of Jesus had been launched as a new and innovative religious order. *O'Malley* 35. Taking the usual vows of chastity, obedience, and poverty made by those entering religious life, the Society's members made an extra vow of obedience to the pope "concerning missions," in this way tying themselves specifically to papal service.

Twenty or more in 1540, the Jesuits had grown to over 3,000 by 1565. *Id.* 36, 51. Led by Ignatius, their charismatic Spanish founder, they incarnated devotion to Christ and to the Church with an energy, a discipline, and an intelligence that made them effective apostles as well as objects of antipathy to their opponents outside the Church and to some within it. By the time the mission to England was begun under the fourth general of the Society, Everard Mercurian, the Jesuits were powerful agents of the Catholic Counter-Reformation, marked by three characteristics that always excite hostility – flexibility, learning, and success. They were a wonderful target on which to train popular suspicion.

In 1580, Edmund Campion and Robert Persons, the first English Jesuits sent to England from abroad, arrived. Anxiety increased in Parliament. "Divers evil-affected persons" were ignoring or evading the earlier law and seeking "to persuade great numbers" to withdraw their obedience to the queen and give it to "the Romish religion."

By 23 Eliz. c.1, these efforts were made high treason, and their non-disclosure by those aware of them, misprision of treason. Penalties for saying mass were introduced (200 marks fine and one year in jail) and for hearing mass (100 marks fine plus a year of jail). The penalties for not attending regular Sunday service were notably increased: 20 pounds for each Sunday missed, one-third to be recoverable by "such person as will sue for the same." So, quietly, a bounty for informers was introduced. The monthly fine alone was 40 to 50 times an artisan's monthly wage. *Haigh* 263. A special penalty was introduced for schoolmasters not attending service: an added 10 pounds fine per service to be paid by the corporate body employing the delinquent and a year of imprisonment for the teacher if convicted.

Campion was captured, tortured, tried, convicted, and executed. Persons escaped abroad. Legislation of 1585 carried the caption, "An Act Against Jesuits, Seminary Priests and other like disobedient Persons," who the statute declared came "to stir up sedition, rebellion, and open hostility"; for them to enter the realm or remain was high treason. 27 Eliz. c.2. The layman who received, relieved, comforted, aided or maintained such a priest was guilty of felony and subject to the death penalty. The statute did not stop the Jesuits or the non-order priests from seminaries such as Douai. In 1586, two notable Jesuits entered England: the poet Robert Southwell and Henry Garnet, destined to lead the Jesuits in England until his execution in 1606. *Caraman* 24.

In 1587, the bite of the law requiring attendance at Sunday service was sharpened. If the delinquent failed to pay the fine of 20 pounds, the government was authorized to take two-thirds of the delinquent's property. 29 Eliz. c.6. For the well-to-do it was an ingenious torment, leaving them enough to feel how much they had lost. It necessarily increased the informer's bounty.

In 1593, an Act against Popish Recusants fine-tuned the law. Parliament took note of "sundry wicked and seditious persons, who terming themselves Catholics and being indeed spies and intelligencers . . . do secretly wander and shift from place to place within this realm, to corrupt and seduce her Majesty's subjects." These recusants, that is, persons refusing to attend the services of the established church, were commanded to stay within five miles of their usual abode and to register their address with the local parish, or forfeit all their property. If they had no property, they should abjure the realm and leave it – a kind of exile being imposed on Catholic paupers. 35 Eliz. c.2.

The term "recusant," first employed by 7 Edw. VI, c.4, was itself derived from a Latin verb *recuso* (to refuse), long in theological use. Schismatics, wrote Thomas Aquinas, "refuse (*recusant*) to communicate with the members and subjects of the Church." *Aquinas*, 2 -2, q.39, art. 1. The verb used by Catholic theologians to characterize Christians out of communion with Rome became a noun neatly turned against Catholics by the legislators who wanted them to be in communion with the Church of England. It was a nicely legal term, not simply abusive but designating those who wilfully refrained from attending the Sunday services of the Church of England.

To make the statutes work, the royal will had to be given force by a determined national leadership. Local zealotry, opportunistic informers, and an alert constabulary were important auxiliaries. Acquiescence was also required in the new state of religious affairs. Pockets of persons committed to the old ways prevented general acquiescence. Even with the encouragement of bounties, informers were insufficient, with the aid of constables more like Dogberry than the F.B.I., to wipe out the Catholics. The popularity and persistence of pilgrimages to St. Winifred's Well illustrate the point.

Winifred was a Welsh girl whose legend was as old as the twelfth century. She was killed when she preferred to honor her vow of virginity to accepting an offer of marriage. *Gerard* 46. Isabella in *Measure for Measure* is a person difficult for modern audiences to identify with, because she puts her virginity above her brother's life. Winifred was of the same cloth. As St. Winifred, she came in legend to preside over a spring in North Wales where miracles took place. *Id.* 47-48. Perhaps because it was far from London, St. Winifred's Well was the object of pilgrimages for Jesuits such as Garnet in 1602. *Caraman* 248.

In August of the fateful year 1605, Garnet made the pilgrimage a second time. On the journey, he stayed with John Grant near Stratford and with Robert Wintour. He was eventually accompanied by John Gerard, Edward Oldcorne, and Oswald Tesimond, all Jesuits; Sir Everard and Lady Digby; Elizabeth Rookwood, the wife of Ambrose; and over a dozen other gentry not counting servants. On "the last stages" of the pilgrimage, the women walked barefoot to the shrine. *Caraman* 325. This Chaucerian cavalcade must have been conspicuous, but no harm then befell the pilgrims. It was only after the events of November 5, 1605 that the suspicious gaze of the government fell upon members of this group, and that Henry Garnet, Sir Everard, John Grant, Ambrose Rookwood, and Robert Wintour were executed, in addition to four others, for their part in the Gunpowder Treason. *Caraman* 248; *Hogge* 341, 359-360.

Gunpowder. In 1605, the third year of King James, the kingdom nearly exploded, and the law did. An Act for the better discovery and repression of Popish Recusancy stated that it was "found by daily experience that many of his Majesty's subjects adhere in their hearts to the Popish Religion." The proof: "the barbarous and horrible attempt to have blown up with gunpowder the King, Queen, Puisne Lords and Commons in the House of Parliament assembled," a plot "lately undertaken by the instigation of Jesuits and Seminaries." To better discover such persons, every convicted recusant was required to receive the sacrament of the Lord's supper at least once a year. The logic of the requirement was that a Catholic feigning conformity would likely balk at the actual reception of the sacrament in the Church of England. The king's power to exact property from recusants was enlarged: the 20-pound fine was extended to include land held in trust for the offender. 3 Jas. c.5. A companion statute, c.4, barred convicted recusants from London and from the court and from being lawyer or judge, apothecary or physician. Any wife convicted of recusancy could not be executor of her husband's estate and must surrender two-thirds of her dowry or jointure. Convicted recusants were to be treated as excommunicates. Recusants were known to be married and buried and to have their children christened not according to the laws of the Church of England. Penalties were set for each of these evasions of the establishment. Provisions were made to search for popish books, then to be burned, and for popish crucifixes, to be defaced and then returned to their owners. Recusants were not to keep armor, gunpowder, or munitions of any kind. In large and small ways the Catholics of England were harassed as if all of them had been privy to the conspiracy to blow up the government. Attorney General Coke, about to become Chief Justice of Common Pleas, summed up the Gunpowder Plot as "the Jesuit treason." *Marotti* 33 quoting p.1 of *A True and Perfect Relation of the proceedings at the several Arrangements of the Late Most Barbarous Traitors, Garnet, a Jesuite and his confederates.*

Remember, Remember

The fifth of November.

So Protestant propaganda was to put it, as Guy Fawkes Day became an annual celebration of the delivery of the nation, and the Gunpowder Plot became a catastrophe for the Catholics of England.

Crushed Community? With the exposure of the Plot, the legislation against Catholics reached a climax. Legal description not of their choosing had been fixed upon them: recusant. "Papist," also employed by the statutes, had been a Lutheran term of abuse since 1521. *O.E.D.* at "papist." In the statutes of England it was a smear connoting a person slavishly subject to the pope.

Identified Catholics were limited in their abodes, banned from London, and even subject to involuntary exile. They were denied a variety of occupations. They were subject to financial ruin. Their priests from abroad became criminals by coming and subject to the death penalty as traitors. They themselves were felons for feeding or housing them and also subject to execution. They were cut off from communication with their own Church and forced to attend services in which they did not believe. They had no space in which to worship unless it were a lax prison or a gentleman's country home. *McClain* 144-147. The scattered centers of Catholic life were marked by "compromise, dissembling and anxiety." *Sweeney* 3. If one can call this oppressed people "a community," as is commonly done, it was a community submerged in a society hostile to its existence.

No resident bishop spoke for it. Henry Garnet, while he was at liberty, had status as the head of the local Jesuits, but he had no jurisdiction outside his order. In 1595, George Blackwell was given by Rome the curious title of "archpriest," but his appointment generated division among Catholics, not obedience. *Caraman*, 239, 300. What did exist were not dioceses or parishes, but Catholic families, entourages, circles. They recognized each other and formed networks. Among them were those who practiced their religion and yet maintained their status with the Crown. The Earl of Worcester is commonly taken as the ranking Catholic at Elizabeth's court. *Finnis and Martin* 13-14. Magdelene Browne, Viscountess Montague, an outspoken woman, kept her Catholicism and her place in society. *Questier* 211-213. No doubt some conformity with the law was necessary for those who passed.

Catholics who conformed were, in hostile eyes, "church papists," and a rigorist among their Catholic co-religionists could have thought them schismatics, Catholics at heart, Anglicans on Sundays. As a modern historian observes, "It is notoriously difficult to quantify and differentiate recusants and church papists." *Heal* 471.

A community that was scarcely a community, whose members sometimes mixed easily with their persecutors, and whose loyalties were often determined by family connections, the Catholics of England between 1590 and 1610 were dependent on the sacerdotal stream that brought them the sacraments from abroad. Catholicism has had memorable mystics. For the larger, more ordinary run of folk, it is experienced more tangibly than in inspired introspection or solitary struggle with the supernatural. It lives in the perfect oblation of the mass – not in homilies or catechisms, not in beautiful pageantry that sometimes catches the eye of the observer on the outside, not in "bells and smells" as high liturgies are cruelly caricatured, but most pertinently in confession and absolution and in the reception of the Eucharist. The delivery of these tangible tokens – and more than tokens, religious realities – has to be made by priests.

Undeterred by being classified as traitors, undeterred by what they might suffer if captured, the priests came. Between 1574 and 1603, a modern historian calculates, 600 priests returned to England from the continent. *Haigh* 261. The majority were imprisoned or deported or first imprisoned and then deported. Incarceration might be at Wisbech Cantle in the country or at one of a dozen London prisons, including cruel Newgate; the Clink where the inmates had minimal supervision; the Tower, a grim fortress; or Bridewell, a hole for vagabonds where a recusant might learn under the lash to tread a treadmill. *Caraman* 195; *Gerard* 83. Of the 600, 129 were put to death. *Haigh* 263.

Any ending of a human being's life by the state is a horror. No one thought so in 1600. The death of a traitor was made as difficult, as humiliating, as painful as possible. The condemned was dragged on a hurdle to a public place of execution; hung by the neck; cut down while still living, castrated and disemboweled; his heart finally held before the crowd, his body quartered, the quarters to be hung on city gates, and his head stuck on a bridge. Those fleshly remains were the body parts observed by John Donne.

Elizabeth's agents did not create the fiery spectacles that Mary's had by burning heretics. They created equally ghastly gallows scenes. They could say that no one died for religion but for violating a valid requirement of national security. They could not change the conviction of those who died that they suffered for Christ or alter the belief of their coreligionists that the hung priests were martyrs for the faith.

The laity suffered death as accomplices, but in lesser number – 36 as of 1592. *Id*. 263. Four women eventually joined this roll of nonclerical martyrs. *Gregory* 280. The laity were hit more often in their property, although the administration of the recusancy fines was chaotic rather than efficient and was marked by evasion and collusion. *Haigh* 263. In 1592, only 142 recusants paid fines to the Exchequer. *Id*. 264. Nonetheless, a chief pursuivant responsible for collecting recusancy fines like Thomas Felton could find it a complicated and lucrative business. *Trimble* 248. No mass slaughter of the sort that disfigured the twentieth century disgraced Elizabethan England. But determined and knowledgeable men were devoted to the destruction of papolatry; their devotion was sometimes mixed, as in the case of Richard Topcliffe, with a malice expressed in cruelty. Robert Southwell could, with a poet's sensibility, describe the desolation of poor, persecuted Catholics in these terms addressed in 1594 to the Queen:

Yea and this law hath been so violently executed that where poor farmers and husbandmen had but one cow for themselves and many children to live upon, that for their recusancy hath been taken from them. And where both kine and cattle were wanting, they have violently taken their coverlets, sheets, and blankets from their beds, their victuals and poor provision from their houses, not sparing so much as the very glass of their windows. *Southwell 1993* 43.

A poet's pen could generalize a single instance. It would be rash to doubt that incidents of this kind occurred; it would be equally rash to suppose that they were common. To express hyperbolically the social status of poets, Donne declares that

> they are poor, disarmed, like papists, not worth hate.
>
>   Donne, *Satires* II.10.

The persecution was selective and episodic, the persecution left wounds, the perseuction laid the persecuted low.

Campion's open letter in 1580 to the Privy Council, popularly known as Campion's "Brag," was an announcement of his apostolic mission. *Miola* 63-75. He declared that the expense of the enterprise undertaken by the Jesuits in England had been "reckoned." *McCoog 2007* xxxii. The Jesuits must have realized that some of them would give their lives in the enterprise. Their faith was such that they were willing to bear this cost. It is hard, however, to see how they could calculate the expense their English hosts might incur in cash, land, or lives.

The Jesuits were instructed to stay out of secular politics. *Caraman* 20-21. But only by regime change would their efforts accomplish much. Without such change, they could nurse the faith of the families they reached, administer the sacraments and occasionally make converts or reconcile the lapsed. They could not effect the conversion of England. It was a constant temptation to turn to worldly measures. The reaction of the government was to increase the pressure.

A feature of the prosecutorial process was torture. Banned by the common law, its use is documented between 1540 and 1640 by virtue of its authorization by warrant of the king, queen or privy council. Commissioners to oversee the application of the torture to a particular prisoner included the Attorney General, Edward Coke, and Francis Bacon at the start of his climb to the chancellorship. *Langbein* 85-86. The Jesuit John Gerard was one of their cases. *Gerard* 106, n.1. Standard tortures were the rack which pulled limbs apart and the manacles which suspended the prisoner with his feet not touching the ground. *Id*. 108-109.

"If an army loyal to the pope invaded England, would you fight for the queen or for the invaders?" This interrogation, known to Catholics as "the bloody question," had relevance in 1588 when the Spanish Armada threatened England with invasion. It was still being asked in 1594 when it posed no more than a hypothetical dilemma and was posed by none other than by the Tower's top torturer, Topcliffe, who relished his fiendish reputation among recusants. *Gerard* 98-99. From the viewpoint of the state, national security was at stake when the loyalty of subjects could be doubted. From the state's standpoint, the question was legitimate as torture was legitimate and as the ultimate penalty for treason like the Gunpowder Plot was legitimate.

The burden of the prosecution was the less as no counsel was provided the defendant. Only the prosecutors were lawyers. And there was no appeal from a verdict of guilty. A jury spoke. A judge gave the sentence. The case was over. Execution of the sentence followed.

Conformity: A Spectrum. Conscientious conformity to secular legislation was generally acknowledged Christian duty if it didn't compel one to sin. Conscientious conformity to the rules of one's religion was part of being religiously observant. As the demands of two different jurisdictions clashed, compromises and evasions, as well as strict compliance with one rule or the other presented themselves to those subject to the spiritual and secular pressures placed by the clashing imperatives. I will suggest the variety of choices possible. I will conclude by pointing to the choices made by two formidable spirits contemporaneous with Shakespeare.

Questions of conscience lay in the realm of religious observance. In *Measure for Measure*, Angelo, with hypocritical hyperbole, compares the generation of a child out of wedlock to the murder of a man: both acts are condemned by heaven's laws. Isabella replies:

'Tis set down so in heaven, but not on earth.

Measure for Measure 2.4.50.

Even the high-principled Isabella knows that the earthly application of laws must be tempered. It may be guessed that her attitude was not uncommon among Catholics confronting the earthly statutes of England and Pius V's rules.

Could a good Catholic attend the required service at the local Church of England parish? Could he or she be married by the local clergyman or have children baptized in the local church or attend a local funeral? The answers, in part, lay in the difference made between what was morally lawful and what was valid. Since at least Gratian's *Concordia discordantium canonum*, circa 1150, this line had been drawn. To partake of a sacrament unlawful because it involved participation in schism or heresy was to sin. To partake of an invalid sacrament was not only sinful but ineffectual; nothing was accomplished. Invalidity was far worse than illegality. This difference is sometimes underplayed by modern commentators. For a practicing Catholic of the Elizabethan age it was substantial. The morally unlawful could be cured by repentance. The invalid was broken beyond repair.

A valid marriage was formed by the unconditional, uncoerced consent of the couple to take each other as man and wife for life. Gratian, *Concordia,* Part II, Causae 31-36. The Council of Trent had added the requirement that the consent to be valid must be exchanged before the parish priest – a serious difficulty for English Catholics. But Trent applied only where its decrees had been promulgated. They had not been promulgated in England or its colonies. As late as 1880, the Tridentine law was not observed in the ecclesiastical provinces of Baltimore, Boston, New York and Philadelphia. Noonan, *Power To Dissolve*, 255.

Catholic theologians taught that baptism could be conferred by any Christian. The validity of baptism in the local church could not be denied. Garnet in 1588 recounted to Aquaviva the story of a pregnant Catholic woman who wanted to avoid the baptism of her child by the local minister; she traveled beyond her county and gave birth in an open field. *Caraman* 90. The story celebrated exceptional conduct. Nothing in the story implies that baptism in a church of the Church of England would have been invalid.

Funerals and burials didn't operate as sacraments. Extreme unction was not essential. Absolution from sin and celebration of the Eucharist were essential and could only be carried out by a clergyman who was validly ordained. Reforms made by the Church of England suggested a ritual incompatible with Catholic requirements for validity, but as of 1600 no pope or Roman congregation had declared Anglican orders to be invalid. A Catholic's problem with the practice of his religion within the walls of the established church was the problem of cooperating in the sin of schism or the sin of heresy.

About 1600 at Louvain, at the command of his superiors, John Gerard wrote a memoir of his mission to England; he had an audience of Jesuit novices from England primarily in mind. *Gerard* xxvii. He recalled how he responded when, a prisoner, he was falsely told that Robert Southwell had capitulated and had accepted the established Church, so he should follow his example. Gerard replied, "I don't keep out of heresy and avoid heretical meetings because he or any other person says so, but because I would be denying Christ by denying the faith." *Gerard* 75. This defiance, and the retelling to the novices, set out an heroic model.

Conformity was addressed professionally by a master moral theologian, Tomás Sanchez, a Jesuit teaching at Cordova between 1580 and 1610, who left a Latin treatise on the ten commandments, published and probably revised after his death. One cannot say with certainty that every conclusion reached in the published work was his. But the stamp of his supple and subtle spirit runs through it. It is good evidence of Jesuit teaching on the continent contemporaneous with Shakespeare. Under the Second Commandment, Sanchez placed the topic "The obligation of external confession of the faith," that is, what a believer must manifest as distinct from the beliefs held in his heart. *Sanchez*, II, q.4, c.27, discussing no specific English statutes but showing a general awareness of the legal position of Catholics in England. He asked, "What if a prince infected by heresy commands all to attend the temples (*templa*) of the heretics under serious penalties of death or deprivation of property?" He broadly distinguished the fulfillment of civil or secular duties from active participation in heretical rites or services. To attend services out of "due obedience" to the law or to listen to the sermons of heretics was not "intrinsically evil" and could be permitted if scandal was not given to fellow Catholics. Catholics might also morally attend such services in the performance of their secular duties – e.g., the swordbearer carrying the sword before the king and, in general, servants attending to their duties to their masters. But there was an important proviso: that the servants not "take part (*communicare*) in the rites and prayers of the heretics." There was where Sanchez saw the line drawn.

In England, he observed, the magistrates required attendance at church "for a most forceful reason," to have the Catholics participate in heretical worship (*cultus*), so that heretics and Catholics could not be distinguished. When they entered a church of the heretics, the Catholics were compelled "to sing, to pray, to kneel in the fashion of the heretics" and thence (*psoinde*) to participate in their rites. "The heretics glory in the flow of Catholics" into their temples, and other Catholic "think themselves deserted." In Scotland, it was even worse: Catholics were led to make actual denial of articles of faith. Acknowledgment of the supreme spiritual power of the king of England within his kingdom, Sanchez concluded, was not permissible for Catholics; similarly it was not lawful for them to attend churches where they become sharers in the services.

This formal analysis incorporated the spirit of the early Christian martyrs and the rigidity of the Counter – Reformation. The contemporary conflict was like the ancient struggle against pagan persecutors. Compromise with iniquity was iniquity.

Sanchez's analysis, on its face, left little wiggle room. Attendance to perform purely secular duties appeared to be unlikely. A Catholic attending a nonCatholic church in England or Scotland appeared to be guilty of sin. As always in Catholic moral theology, overarching principles modified such a hard conclusion; for example, no one is bound by a moral rule he does not know. The law of the realm was clear and harsh. A moral obligation to disobey it could seem not only difficult but cloudy. In practice, areas of moral ignorance could exist.

Assume that some English Catholics convinced themselves that they could feign conformity with the establishment. The question then becomes, Is ignorance excusable or crass and therefore not excused? As to individual Catholics caught in the conflict between their faith and the requirements of conformity, it would be hazardous to judge their conduct by the criteria set out in the seminaries.

Sanchez wrote for other professional theologians, secondarily for scholarly confessors. That his judgments were mediated in transmission is a fair probability. He himself wrote that the conclusion of his analysis "could not be turned into doubt." Did not this way of putting it suggest that it was doubted by others? Sanchez spoke without qualification of "the heretics." Gerard in his memoir had distinguished a heretic from a schismatic; the latter was one who, Catholic in belief, attended a Protestant church. *Gerard* 135. A tough-minded Catholic might have convinced himself that his part in Anglican worship was merely the performance of a civic obligation. It was one thing for Sanchez to write for fellow professionals or for Gerard to instruct the novices, and another matter to minister to the harassed Catholics of England.

What was taught in safety in a seminary on the continent was, in fact, literally repeated in books brought to England and was, in fact, liberally diluted in practice. The logic of the theologians led one way. The circumstances pointed the opposite way.

Lines as sharp and clear as Sanchez's were drawn by Marian clergy who had been ousted from office under Elizabeth – e.g., John Young, once the Master of Pembroke Hall and the Professor of Divinity at Cambridge. *Holmes* 85. It was not just the dispossessed who demanded that Catholics not conform. It was the message of the missionaries – for example, Robert Persons in 1580 in *A brief discourse containing certain reasons why Catholics refuse to go to church* and Henry Garnet in

1593 in *A treatise of Christian renunciation*. *Id*. William Allen sounded the same call as the Jesuits. *Id*. 107.

Not every Catholic moralist agreed with the hard line. A strategically placed defender of conformity was Allen Langdale, a Marian priest deprived of his office as archdeacon of Chicester, who had become the chaplain of Anthony Browne, Viscount Montague, a leading Catholic peer. Langdale's defense was circulated, persuading some members of the nobility to attend Anglican services. *Id*. 90. Thomas Bell, a seminary priest at work in Lancaster in the early 1590's, was another defender of this position of particular importance to the Catholic gentry of Lancaster. *Id*. 95. More significant are records of conferences of theologians held before the students at the English college at Rheims, exploring the cases in which Catholic presence at an Anglican service might be permitted. At one such deliberation in 1571, it was agreed that Catholics who did so out of the fear that coerces a steady man were not excommunicated for their attendance. *Id*. 103. Another document from the early 1580's at Rheims was signed off on by both William Allen and Robert Persons. It discussed as permissible what a modern author calls "occasional conformity" – for example when traveling. The desirability of keeping "noble and rich families" in the faith and of avoiding their "ruin" was expressly noted. *Id*. 102-103. Church attendance was admitted to be morally lawful when such attendance was absolutely necessary so long as it was infrequent. *Id*. 104. The thrust of the discussion was pastoral and practical. The theologians did not want every English Catholic to risk ruin. The tone was not that of Gerard speaking to the Louvain novices or of Sanchez summing up for other moral theologians. If the discussions at Rheims are indicative, the likelihood is that the moral demands made by the Catholic clergy in person were adapted to circumstance and understood by the laity in ways varying from the

rigorist to the lax. The majority adopted the position recommended in
a poem entitled "The Lookers-on":

> In worldly works degrees are three,
>
> Makers, doers and lookers-on:
>
> The lookers-on have liberty,
>
> Both the others to judge upon.
>
> Wherefore in all, as men are bent,
>
> See all, say nought, hold thee content.

Heywood 186

The lines are ambiguous. They begin with a reference to "worldly
works," apparently excluding churchly rites. But "lookers-on"
is a phrase from the *Book of Common Prayer.* Line five speaks
comprehensively of "in all." The author of *The Lookers-on* was Jasper
Heywood, a descendant of Thomas More, an uncle of John Donne,
and a Jesuit. Captured, tortured, and expelled from England; he was
kept from returning to the English mission because he was out of step
with the militant Robert Persons. *McCoog* (2007) 247. Are his lines to
be read as a defense of necessary conformity or do they mock it? Does
Heywood convey an Erasmian broadness, or is he asking his readers to
do more than look? The ambiguity of the verse suggests how hard it
was to condemn the conformity forced upon the citizenry.

Why didn't Pius V's bull, *Regnans in excelsis* decide the question
of conscience? *Regnans in excelsis*, Pius V's excommunication of
Elizabeth, had been a declaration of war. It denounced the impiety
and wickedness of the queen. It proclaimed her a heretic. It deprived
her of her "pretended" right to rule. It excommunicated anyone who
adhered to her. "Let no one dare to obey her or any of her directions,
laws, or commands," the pope commanded. If any did, he, too, came
under the pope's ban. *Miola* 486-488. No attempt had been made in
Rome to give the queen a hearing. Her obduracy in sin was manifest

at least to the pope's advisers on the affairs of England. Taken to the letter, *Regnans in excelsis* disabled all Catholics from serving Elizabeth. A Catholic with a scrupulous conscience was compelled to choose between obeying the pope or the queen, or so it might seem.

Regnans in excelsis, however, was positive papal legislation. It had not been promulgated in England. What counted as to conscience was the moral law as interpreted by theologians, confessors, and by community practice. Conscience does not exist in a vacuum cutting off the community. And the community was divided.

It is a temptation for anyone writing history to depend on what is most available – in this case, the formal treatises on moral behavior. Experience in one's own time and tradition teaches that all kinds of formal rules may be subordinated to the habits of ordinary life and the pressures to conform to the practices of one's contemporaries. For that reason, Sanchez and Gerard are imperfect guides to what anyone in Shakespeare's position thought or did.

What Catholics actually did was not all that secular statutes or their own religious authorities prescribed. One may think of the teaching on contraception today or the conduct of many Catholics in Communist China. To use a German proverb that my Boalt colleague Dick Buxbaum quotes: "Die Suppe wird nicht so heiss gegessen wie gekocht" or "You cook it hotter than you eat it." Moral theology in print was hotter than its application on the ground in England. I see no evidence, for example, that William Byrd, a Catholic deep in providing music for the Church of England, was treated as an open sinner by his Jesuit friends.

Byrd's life affords an eminent example of how a man of unusual genius and Catholic convictions could survive and flourish in Elizabeth's England. He first appears as an organist at Lincoln Cathedral and is suspected of sympathy for the pope. *Kerman 2001* 714. He moves to the court where he is made a gentleman of the Chapel Royal and writes music in praise of Elizabeth. He's given a patent conferring on him a monopoly of printed music in England. But in a report to the government in 1580, he is listed among "relievers of papists and conveyers of money to them." *Id.*, 718. Nothing is done to him. John Reason (a singer and his servant), his own daughters Elizabeth and Rebecca, and his wife are each indicted for recusancy; only the servant is jailed. Ultimately, he himself is cited several times as a recusant and ordered to respond in court to the repeated charges. Each time the case is quashed by the express intervention of the queen or the attorney-general. *Mateer* 1-12.

Byrd appears to enjoy personal immunity. He still has to be careful. He does not openly proclaim his faith or scorn the establishment. He uses Aesopian means, often musical settings of the psalms, to express his sorrow at the situation of his Church. He even writes abroad to the Kapellmeister of the emperor in the same cautious way, in biblical verse lamenting the times: "How should I sing the Lord's song in a strange land?" *Kerman* 2006.

Yet in these distressing circumstances, he is not afraid to be at a house party welcoming the coming of Henry Garnet and Robert Southwell to England, criminals though they become by the very act of coming. Almost twenty years later, in June of 1605, four months before the exposure of the Gunpowder Plot, he is again glimpsed in the company of Garnet. *Kerman 1981* 50. Some of his compositions are read by Philip Brett, the modern editor of his works, as expressing his feelings at what for him were martyrdoms and the mocking of the remains of the martyrs. *Brett* 124.

The horrors happened. According to one account, Barkworth and Filcock, two priests hanged along with Anne Line in 1601, sang out at Tyburn the music Byrd supplied for *Haec dies quam Dominus fecit*.

Later Byrd wrote a four-piece musical setting for Filcock's last words. *Manson* 363. Byrd wrote unabashedly in honor of St. Peter, "shepherd of the sheep, teacher of the church, guardian of the flock." "*Beatus Petrus*" in *Tudor Church Music* 270-271. He kept on writing masses and motets for liturgies to be performed in the households of the Catholic gentry. His *Gradualia* were a whole set of liturgical compositions, the first volume of which consists of music for the feasts of Mary and for the Saturday masses in her honor. In 1605, a Byrd hymn proclaimed:

> *Maria Virgo cunctas haereses sola interemistic*

In English:

> O Virgin Mary, you alone have crushed all heresies.
>
> > *Miola* 313.

Other of his writings were for Corpus Christi and its glorification of the real presence of Christ in the Eucharist.

Byrd could be understood as a deeply divided soul, or as an ecumenicist, or as a person purposeful in his religious goals, flexible enough to accommodate himself to the occasion. He cannot be understood as a man who took *Regnans in excelsis* literally or accepted without question moralists like Gerard or Sanchez. A modern authority on him, Joseph Kerman, describes him as "exceedingly toughminded." *Kerman 2001*, 717. Committed to the Catholic faith, he escaped the censures of the law, served the queen as a composer, and still wrote copiously in honor of the queen of heaven and her son.

Byrd, fellow of the Royal Chapel, celebrant of the Queen, by royal authority monopolist of music, is also the maker of music for masses, the celebrant of martyrs, the companion of Catholic criminals. The survival, the prosperity of a Byrd depended on his knowing the rules – not the statutes of the realm, not anything clearly defined by custom, but limits and boundaries and opportunities that an armed and agile mind, attentive to the ways of his environment, would guess. His path does not demonstrate but suggests the course that Shakespeare could have taken.

At the other end of the spectrum of Catholic lights in the Age of Elizabeth was Robert Southwell, S.J. Southwell was the grandson of a man who had profited from the confiscation of the monasteries. His father was part of the court of the queen. His mother's side of the family had distinctly Catholic leanings. In defiance of the law, he left England to study in Rome and become a Jesuit. He returned to England as a missionary, to bring the truth, as he wrote his father, to those dearest to him. *Southwell, Records*, I 339-347. Coming back, he was a criminal and a hunted man. He ran before the hounds like the agile hare in Shakespeare's *Venus and Adonis*. While he was hunted, he wrote explicitly Catholic poetry, which was clandestinely published. Unlike Byrd, he could not collaborate with the establishment or mix with the court. Yet he had the chutzpah or the sense of belonging with the privileged to write the queen directly on behalf of his persecuted co-religionists. Even after his capture and imprisonment he did not hesitate to write to Robert Cecil, a dominant power in the queen's government, who, of course, knew his father and remarked on the son's suffering but who had no known sympathy for Catholics. In the vocabulary of modern security forces, Southwell was a high value prisoner and therefore an inviting prospect for torture. Betrayed, imprisoned, and repeatedly tortured, Southwell sustained the ordeal and accepted execution as a joy.

Less than fifteen years after *Regnans in excelsis* had excommunicated Elizabeth and released her subjects from any obligation to obey her, Southwell sent a letter to her, addressing her as "Most mighty and most merciful, most feared and most beloved Princess." He went on to declare that Catholics were her "loyal subjects." *Southwell. A Humble Supplication In Her Majesty*, p.1.

Southwell's stance on the legitimacy of the government was at odds with that of Robert Persons and other Jesuits. See R.C. Bald, "Introduction to Southwell," *A Humble Supplication*, p. xxiii. His book was condemned by Rome seventeen years after the martyr's death. *Id.* xviii. Speaking in the *Supplication* of "the most sacred title of their most honored Queen" and ending with a prayer that God "prosper and preserve" her, *Supplication*, p. 1, p.46, Southwell said nothing of the queen's role in religion. He went as far as he could and then shut up or as he more decorously put it in "Scorne not the Leaste."

And silent sees that speech could not amend.

"Scorns not the Laste,"

St. Robert, p. 60.

Was the intrepid missionary lying? Had the Jesuit forgotten the fulminations of Pius V? Was he unaware of the teaching of Jesuit moralists like Sanchez? The answer to each of these questions must be an unqualified No. A man on the way to martyrdom does not forget his foundations. Southwell had reason to consider *Regnans in excelsis* not binding on him in England. The bull had not been promulgated there. It did not prevent a Jesuit missionary from acknowledging Elizabeth as his monarch. The disagreement demonstrates the difficulty of determining where a conscientious Catholic had to draw the line.

Southwell and Byrd by their conduct demonstrate what a conscientious Catholic in Elizabethan England could conscientiously do. Between the martyr and the musician there may be a third man: William Shakespeare. He had to have known both. Did he stand within the community that included both inside its spectrum? In all Shakespeare's work the Society of Jesus is never mentioned nor is any of its members named. He is never seen in their company. "Papist," a common term of abuse, reinforced by its statutory usage, occurs only once in Shakespeare and then in the mouth of Lavatch

[= LaVache = The Cow]. Spewing biblical phrases, he is "a foul-mouthed and calumnious fool" in the words of the Countess of Roussillon. *All's Well That Ends Well* 1.3.49-50. The bloody question is never asked, although think of the question Lear asks his daughters. *King Lear* 1.1.42-45. The England in which Shakespeare sets his comedies is untroubled by religious persecution. Recusancy is a crime and a word unmentioned by him. No pursuivant becomes rich by netting his share of a recusancy fine. It is scarcely strange that most of the critical writing on Shakespeare says nothing of Jesuits, recusants, pursuivants. If Shakespeare never got involved, if he were another looker-on, why call up scenes and issues that he avoided? Why identify him with the precarious community?

3. *Markers*

<u>Bias and biographers</u>. Shakespeare is an idol of our culture. His status within it is supported by a projection of our own ideals. It is notorious that Shakespeare, being found to be all things to all men, his plays have been seen through the eyes of each beholder. My colleague David Daube, himself an emigre from Germany, once superbly caricatured the critics by proving that Shakespeare's plays had originally been written in German. *Daube*, 183-186.

Nowhere has the force of a critic's convictions been more evident than in writing about Shakespeare's religious beliefs or world view. For three centuries it was accepted that he was an Anglican. A favorite image that probably reached its zenith with the Puseyites was that of an Anglican of the middle way. The blurring of lines that let "church papists" go undetected or undeterred was responsible in later times for the conviction that a man of moderation, such as Shakespeare was supposed to be, would not have held beliefs that were anathema to Anglicanism. This conviction is too comfortable to have completely disappeared.

That dominant picture was, however, effectively challenged by those like Matthew Arnold who imbibed the religious disillusionment of some eminent Victorian intellectuals and so could write of Shakespeare,

> Others abide our question; thou art free.
>
> We ask and ask – Thou smilest and sit still
>
> *Arnold* 2.

Free apparently from all religious commitments.

The attribution of agnosticism has persisted into modern criticism and has only grown stronger. It is a superior position, once it is accepted that religious belief is a prejudice. The critic appears as free of the biases of religious people. He or she is alone impartial. So Shakespeare's impartial, above all religious cast and commitment.

Caricature of this kind is too harsh to apply to all who are agnostic as to Shakespeare's religion. Their reticence to commit themselves can reflect puzzlement, an awareness of the limitations on our knowledge of the man. Limitations loom particularly large when one thinks of the active mind of Shakespeare responding to the spiritual, intellectual and political currents of his turbulent time. To chart the precise course of his beliefs exceeds our capacity.

No one is free from views on the nature of the world, our fate within it, and our fate after our lives are over – not Shakespeare, not those who have celebrated his apparent absence of commitments. No one – agnostic, Anglican, atheist, Buddhist, or Catholic – is preserved immaculately from a point of view in these things. No doubt, each thinks his standpoint has a special strength. The impossibility of neutrality should be admitted and not allowed to prevent consideration of the evidence. Someone must be right about Shakespeare as to his beliefs reflected in a particular composition at a particular time.

In the 1930's, writing of Shakespeare's relation to Catholicism, G. B. Harrison observed. "Until recent years religious partisanship has been so strong in England that it has hardly been possible for such a question to be examined without heat." Harbison in *Chambrun vi.* Over half a century later, Gary Taylor wrote: "Even in our ecumenical era, many of Shakespeare's most enthusiastic readers would recoil from the vision of a papist bard; in earlier periods the concept would have been even more difficult to entertain. As one eighteenth-century

Englishman declared, 'tis absurd to suppose; 'tis impossible for any man to imagine'." *Taylor* 291, taking the quotation from a 1752 issue of *Gentleman's Magazine*, the prototype of politically correct periodicals.

A "vision of a papist bard" continued to cause recoil in the twentieth century. Two German scholars in the 1950's produced a study translated as *Shakespeare and Catholicism*. It caused no reassessment by Englishmen. In 1973, Peter Milward put forward a case for Shakespeare as an adult remaining a Catholic. His work was largely ignored, chiefly. I believe, because Milward was himself a Jesuit and therefore suspected of parti pris. Three more recent writers have been conspicuous in going further and contending for the Catholicism entrenched in some of Shakespeare's plays. Velma Richmond has given a luminous reading of the late plays by finding a Catholic glow within. She sees the four plays that are classified as romances as structural expressions of a Catholic habit of mind, showing patient suffering of God's will that leads ultimately to joy. *Richmond* 15-18. The four plays are *Pericles, Prince of Tyre*, of which Acts I and II are attributed to George Wilkins, see *Vickers 2002*, p. 330, and the more familiar *Cymbeline, The Winter's Tale* and *The Tempest*. In Shakespeare's section of *Pericles*, for example, Marina who has been kidnaped by pirates and sold to a brothel, declares her devotion to virginity with a vigor equal to Isabella's in *Measure for Measure*, see *Pericles* 16, 130-131. In the pagan setting of the play, her patron is the virgin goddess Diana. Her story follows Christian hagiographic tradition. She keeps her vow and converts her customers, just as in the life of St. Agatha she was given to a brothel keeper and remained pure, and in *The Golden Legend* St. Agnes makes a brothel an oratory, and St. Katherine surmounts similar circumstances, a teacher with eloquence. *Richmond* 164; *Duffy* 175. In the play Marina is a saint for Shakespeare, a saint unlikely to beguile modern minds.

Clare Asquith, with the boldness of a writer not seeking tenure, has proposed a sweeping allegorical rereading of many of the nonhistorical plays. Her approach is least persuasive when applied to the great tragedies but stimulating when applied to plays that no one has been able to make anything of. Is more light gained by saying with T.S. Eliot that *Titus Andronicus* is "one of the stupidest and most uninspired plays ever written" *Maus* 371, or to find, as Asquith does, this tale of raw and reciprocal cruelties an allegory? As allegory, the lack of mercy shown by Titus to the son of the Queen of the Goths stands for the unthinking rigidity of the old Church under Mary. In the play, at 1.1.23, Titus is surnamed "Pius." It has been suggested that this designation, uniquely in Shakespeare, is meant to recall the inquisitor who became Pius V and whose excommunication of Elizabeth brought the papacy and England to open war. *Klause 2008,* 142. Titus' uncompromising stand generates the wild resentments that lead to the rape and silencing of Lavinia, a figure for the despoiled soul of England. The barbarians cut out her tongue so that she cannot denounce the outrage, a symbol of the silencing of the Catholics of England. The fall of Titus and his family represents the fate of the old Catholics. The rule of Tamora and her circle represents the ascendant establishment. *Asquith* 91-99.

Asquith does not give weight to the demonstration by Vickers that Act 1 and probably three other scenes (2.1, 2.2, and 4.1) were by George Peels. See *Vickers 2002*, p. 243. But in the portions of the play undoubtedly owed to Shakespeare Lucius addresses Lavinia, deprived of both hands and tongue.

Speak, gentle sister, who hath martyred thee?

Titus Andronicus 3.1.50.

The Norton edition glosses "martyred" as "violated." The gloss does not capture the resonances of martyrdom in Elizabeth's England.

The central place of the verb is underlined by Titus as he looks on his daughter:

> Nor tongue to tell me who hath martyred thee.
>
> *Id.* 3.1.107.

The ferocity of the assault on Lavinia and the macabre revenge taken by Titus could be read as reflecting Shakespeare's sensibility stretched to rage by the horrors he has known his friends to suffer. The play would also reflect the playwright's consciousness that the Catholics' intolerance had brought about their present predicament.

The pioneers, as a saying of the Old West has it, are the ones with the arrows in their backs. Asquith's effort was savagely attacked in the *New York Review* by a fellow of Trinity College, Cambridge, minor errors were pounced on, major points ignored, her thesis was too gross for rational debate. *Barton* 23.

The work of Richard Wilson, professor of Renaissance Studies at Lancaster University, has found Catholic allusions throughout Shakespeare. Few writers have so drenched themselves in his work. The abundance of Wilson's observations makes both the strength and weakness of his case. Is there so much to be seen below the surface? His case is strongest when he gives particular details unnoticed before. But the same reviewer who attacks Asquith mocks her and Wilson as Baconian-like cryptographers and never for a moment mentions the evidence that points to Shakespeare's hidden faith. Wilson's work has left most mainstream critics unmoved. *Greenblatt* 297 notes its existence and goes on without responding to it. Other standard studies such as James Shapiro's *A Year in the Life of Shakespeare* do not bother to note it. In 2007, a biographer of Shakespeare hovered on the edge of the Jesuit connection, referring to Campion, Garnet, Persons, and Southwell. *Weis* 177-178, 225-226. The connection was not made. The centuries-old portrait of Shakespeare had not been altered enough for conventional critics, much less high school or even college teachers, to notice.

From the European continent a different note was occasionally sounded. For example, a Shakespeare scholar at the Sorbonne effectively challenged a standard English classification of Montaigne as a sceptic, with whose scepticism Shakespeare identified. She notes that in *Cymbeline* Shakespeare reflects Montaigne's *L'Apologie de Raymond Sebond*. Translated into English in 1602, the work set out faith as superior to a skeptical and destructive reason. In turning to "the Roman Catholic Montaigne," Shakespeare was "establishing transconfessional connections" between Catholic and Protestant writers who "were waging their own war against the wars of religion." *Jones-Davies* 202.

A German scholar of Shakespeare, Hildegard Hammerschmidt-Hummel, professor of English Language and Cultural Studies at the University of Mainz, has made the bold claim that Shakespeare registered as a pilgrim under a pseudonym at the English College in Rome in 1585. *Hammerschmidt-Hummel*, 80.

Back in England, within the enclosure of the Shakespeare establishment, such revisionism was not welcomed. The silence on Shakespeare's religion is particularly striking in *Shakespeare & Co.* (2006) by Stanley Wells. The book is devoted to a study of Shakespeare and the collaborators with him and each other. Wells surely knew *Loves Martyr*, published in 1601, to which Shakespeare and Ben Jonson each contributed a poem. If any book deserves to be attributed to *Shakespeare & Co.*, this one requires consideration. Wells mentions the contribution of neither. In its moral seriousness, Jonson's poem is deemed by his biographers to be worthy of comparison with Sonnet 129. "Th' expense of spirit in a waste of shame." *Herford and Simpson* II, 403. In the Oxford Authors series the editor extracted two short selections from it. *Donaldson* 416-417. It is not a trivial contribution to the collaboration in which Shakespeare's part, as Chapter Three will show, is extraordinary. In 1597, Jonson had become a convert to Catholicism. *Wells* 134. *Loves Martyr* presents the opportunity to compare Jonson's work on a subject that appeared within the same covers as Shakespeare's. Wells says not a word.

A recent book bearing the comprehensive title *Shakespeare and Religion* is focused on the plays and does not address the poems considered in Chapters 3 through 12 of this book. Unsurprisingly, it finds that the plays do not demonstrate his Catholicism, noting that the bard's reserve was criticized by two militant but anonymous Catholic contemporaries. Shell, p. 105.

One mainstream critic, Gary Taylor, co-editor with Wells of the current Oxford edition of Shakespeare, has concluded that Shakespeare was a Catholic in his maturity. He writes, "I cannot prove that Shakespeare was a Catholic. But then if he were one, he would have had strong incentives to prevent anyone from being able to prove it. And the hypothesis that he was a Catholic will, I believe, account for all the relevant facts in both the biographical and the literary record." *Taylor* 298.

Taylor discounted the lack of any recusancy charge against Shakespeare: it could be largely explained by his shifting between Stratford and London. *Id.* 297. Sensibly, Taylor points out that within any opposition there are further divisions: "Shakespeare, seeing himself as a moderate Catholic, opposes Cardinal Pandolf." *Id.* 294. The case for Shakespeare's religion is confirmed for Taylor by contrasting it with the Puritanism of the plays of Richard Middleton. Tongue in cheek, after speaking of the old adamancy against admitting Shakespeare to be a Catholic, Taylor remarks, "But I am sure that no one now reading this essay [in *English Literary Renaissance*] harbors — or would admit to harboring – such prejudices." *Id.* 296.

Advancing the claim that Shakespeare was a Catholic poet and playwright, Taylor finds it necessary to disarm his critics by stating that not only is he himself no Catholic, he is no Christian, adding the possibly irrelevant detail that he lost his own faith before he lost his virginity and expects to recover neither. *Taylor* 288. It may be that emphasis is needed if he is not to be assailed as a modern papist. Undoubtedly, the crumbling of old convictions and agreed-on conventions has led to opening of doors once closed and guarded. But citadels of secularism exist. That a confession of religious indifference should now be expected, that such professed conformism with the prevailing intellectual culture should be de rigeur is disquieting; no, it is disgusting.

Taylor seemed to step out of the secular citadel. He was still within its walls. Shakespeare might, so far as he could tell, be a Catholic. His religion was irrelevant. Not the man but the work was what spoke to us. Catholicism was without impact on the plays. The playwright had transmuted "real grief" and "real sacrifice" into "an apparently secular commodity." He had "created the scriptures for an emergent secular world." *Taylor, 2003*, 255-256. What did it matter what he may have thought, Shakespeare gave us what we as modern unbelievers wanted. Snippets and structures. "The proof is in his plays," shouts James Tyrone, the old Shakespearean actor, replying in *A Long Day's Journey Into Night* to his son Edmund, who twits him on his foolish fantasy that Shakespeare was a Catholic. *O'Neill*, Act 4. But the plays are neither a creed nor a catechism. The reading of the whole structure of a play is an art, whose practice is unlikely to provide proof convincing to everyone but enough to excite further inquiry.

For generations, Shakespeare was presented as a pillar of the Elizabethan establishment, the most patriotic of Englishmen, celebrating his country as this sceptered isle . . .

This other Eden, this demi-paradise . . .

This happy breed of men, this little world,

This precious stone set in the silver sea.

Richard II 2.1.40-47.

These prophesying words of the dying Gaunt could be taken from the play and read as the poet's eulogy of England, words utterly appropriate for an author contented at being conventionally baptized, married and buried by the Church of England. He had also provided words to taunt the pope:

no Italian priest

Shall tithe or toll in our dominions.

King John 3.1.78-79

In *All Is True* (known since 1623 as *Henry VIII*), the play ended with the celebration of the birth of Elizabeth and succession by James. What more could a patriotic Protestant do to show his loyalty to crown and church?

These considerations rest on the assumption that the characters speak for the author. The assumption is hazardous. The bad habit of plucking quotations out of plays as plums is carried to a *reductio ad absurdum* when modern Americans, outraged by the antics of a lawyer, cry, "The first thing we do, let's kill all the lawyers," invoking Shakespeare's endorsement of this sentiment in 2 *Henry VI* 4.2.68 and ignoring the fact that it is the utterance of a nameless butcher, a follower of the lying braggart Jack Cade, who dying is denounced as a "damned wretch." *Id.* 5.1.74. A contextual reading of the anti-lawyer battle cry would be that lawyers were hated by ignoramuses.

To attribute to Shakespeare personally the butcher's abuse of the legal profession is a minor error in critical judgment. A major error is that committed in comment on Gloucester's terrible words:

As flies to wanton boys are we to the gods.

They kill us for their sport

King Lear 4.1.37-38.

I was schooled, as have been many, to think these lines do express the mature Shakespeare's views at the time he wrote: a hopeless, rebellious despair of any divine providence guiding us. It is a reflection that has occurred to any experienced observer of the world and of course to Shakespeare. But does it express his settled view of the universe? These words are wrung from Gloucester whose eyes have been violently removed. The cries of a man blinded by human cruelty are not to be taken as the belief of Gloucester's creator.

Gloucester's angry assault on the gods may be set off against Hamlet's dying declaration to Horatio:

There's a divinity that shapes our ends,

Rough-hew them though we will

Hamlet 5.2.10-11

Does Gloucester or does Hamlet speak for Shakespeare? Each speaks for himself. Undoubtedly, what is said by any character in any play incorporates a piece of the author's experience. Personally or vicariously, the author has known the emotions expressed. The author's experiences need to be distinguished from the author's beliefs.

The characters speak in character. Shakespeare provides the lines dramatically appropriate to express character and to create conflict. The playwright's preference for drama is reinforced in the historical plays by his respect for his sources, used selectively but faithfully. His caricature of Joan of Arc in *1 Henry VI* is notorious: he followed the histories he knew. *Nuttall* 34; Joan was canonized only in 1920. If there are crafty cardinals or simoniacal prelates in the historical narratives, Shakespeare does not airbrush them out. *Knapp* 50. To a mature believer, it is no surprise that there are high-placed sinners. The Gospel puts three – Judas, Peter, and Thomas – as the daily companions of Jesus. Dante set Boniface VIII in hell. To read King John's defiance of tribute to Rome as Shakespeare's belief is to see Shakespeare speaking in such slimy characters as Iago. *King John* as a whole is not a paean to an English patriot: John is depicted as a murderer and an usurper. With wonderful dexterity the playwright puts on the right mask as he writes for each of his creations. The same rule holds true when a character speaks well of religion or uses religious language.

A recent close reading of the history plays of Shakespeare, comparing them with others of this genre, notes a sequence reflecting changes in the playwright's perspective and asks: "Does it [the sequence] suggest strengthening recusant sympathies on Shakespeare's part? Does it reveal, beneath the surface of aesthetic innovation, an enduring and sympathetic engagement with the issues raised by, even perhaps the causes of, reformed religion? Or, on the other hand, does it imply a movement of fastidious withdrawal on Shakespeare's part from the disclosure of confessional loyalties of any kind? These are questions which I believe we cannot answer." *Womersley*, p.11. This refusal to force the evidence, this serene acceptance of limitations on our knowledge, has a great deal to recommend it.

But does not every rule have an exception? What if a passage in a play is unrelated to any action, conflict, or manifestation of character? Does not sheer gratuitousness suggest that the passage requires a different treatment?

Mary, Queen of Scots, was a heroine to the Catholics in England. A Catholic poet could not have kept silent about her, especially when she was slandered by a Protestant poet, Edmund Spenser in Book V, Canto 9, of *The Faerie Queen*. Shakespeare did not keep silent. Instead, unexpectedly and unnecessarily as far as the dramatic action is concerned, he paid her tribute in *A Midsummer Night's Dream*. Oberon speaks to Robin with a question:

> Thou rememb'rest
>
> Since once I sat upon a promontory
>
> And heard a mermaid on a dolphin's back
>
> Uttering such dulcent and harmonious breath
>
> That the rude sea grew civil at her song
>
> And certain stars shot madly from their spheres
>
> To hear the mermaid's music?
>
> *A Midsummer Night's Dream* 2.1.148-154

The key to the passage is the dolphin. It is Shakespeare's ordinary spelling in the history plays for dauphin, the heir apparent to the French throne. Mary, once queen of France, entered into power as the bride of the dauphin. In Scotland, she quelled the tumultuous opposition. The earls of Northumberland and Westmoreland and the duke of Norfolk shot out of their spheres by rebelling to put her on the English throne. In five lines, without mention of her name, she is gracefully saluted. *Noonan 2001* 85. Mary was idealized on the Catholic continent. In England, it may be doubted that any non-Catholic would have memorialized her this way.

Fragments of Shakespeare's experience, imaginatively incorporated into drama, a critic may conclude, but is there anything deeper? In *Measure for Measure*, religious argument, entirely suited to the character who makes it, is delivered. With eloquence and theological exactness, its heroine puts the case for mercy:

> Why, all the souls that were were forfeit once,
>
> And He that might the vantage best have took
>
> Found out the remedy. How would you be
>
> If He which is the top of judgment should
>
> But judge you as you are?
>
> Isabella to Angelo, *Measure for Measure* 2.2. 75-79.

The play goes on to examine the meaning of redemption:

Isabella: How now I'll bribe you; good my lord, turn back.

Angelo: How bribe me?

Isabella: Ay, with such gifts that heaven shall share with you.

2.2.148-150.

Angelo continues to seek her body as a bribe, and she responds:

Lawful mercy.

Is nothing kin to foul redemption.

2.4.113-114.

It is possible, I think, to look at Angelo and Isabella's exchanges as a theological probe: a thoughtful believer is asking, "How does redemption differ from the bribing of a judge?" Given the common Christian reading of "redemption," the question is profound. Is the whole story of salvation a payoff to a Judge who accepts the death of His Son as a suitable sacrifice? Still, the exchanges add to the drama and so I would not read the pondering of a central Christian concept as proof of Shakespeare's Catholic belief.

The Duke's decision not to execute the unrepentant Bernardine reflects the theology of mercy that St. Augustine expresses in his letter to Marcellinus on the treatment of the Donatists. See *Shuger* 109-115. It is the same theology that stays Hamlet from killing Claudius at prayer. The state of a man's soul at death determines his destiny beyond his life. Here this theology almost gratuitously contributes a scene to the play.

There is more in *Measure for Measure*. In the final act, Isabella forgives Angelo and kneels to ask the Duke to pardon him. Her act of mercy redeems Angelo. So, as in Matthew 7:1, measure matches measure. Forgiveness leads to forgiveness. It is difficult for me to believe that Shakespeare would have embraced this theme unless he were a believing Christian. That does not mark Shakespeare specifically as a Catholic Christian. It does point to an author whose own spirit has put a premium on redemption. Not that the exchanges take place between Isabella and Angelo on bribery, not that the Duke assumes the robe and role of a Franciscan friar is the play a Christian work. What stamps it such is the entire thrust of the play, carrying the words of Christ as its title, celebrating the primacy of love in acts of redemptive mercy.

All Is True, more pageant than play, with its provocative title, is structured as an effort to do justice both to the old religion and the newly established one. A collaboration, the play has parts undoubtedly written by John Fletcher. *Vickers 2002*, p. 367. The play presents skeletal, sanitized segments of the life of Henry VIII, who had to be treated carefully: he had not only fathered the Church of England, but was also the great-uncle of Mary, Queen of Scots, mother of James I. The play is not polemical. Cardinal Wolsey dominates the first three acts, his good and bad judiciously assessed. The annulment that is pronounced by Cranmer is mentioned but not presented.

Act 4, scene 2 presenting Katherine's last hours, is attributed to Fletcher. *Id.* The scene is interrupted by a silent show in which Katherine is enraptured by a vision of six persons garlanded, robed in white and carrying palms, in short, martyrs. She herself is suggested to be a kind of martyr, rewarded with a foretaste of paradise. Analogously, in a seventeenth century "Book of Martyrs," the story is recounted of St. Anne Line, that while in prison, waiting the day of execution, she heard music no one else heard and saw a light visible to no one else. *Liber martyrorum* at *Mistress Anne Line*. In this way a martyr was believed to have an anticipation of her blessed future. Whether Shakespeare or Fletcher introduced the vision here is open to argument.

The same play in lines believed to be Fletcher's, reaches its near climax with the birth of Elizabeth, who

Though in her cradle, promises

Upon this land a thousand thousand blessings.

5.4.18-19

Cranmer continues over-the-top: Elizabeth is like

the maiden phoenix, when she dies

she shall leave her blessedness to one

Who shall star-like rise as great in fame as she was.

5.4.46

In this star-like character, the reigning monarch, James I, the play reaches its conclusion. *All Is True* may be seen as both a eulogistic and an ecumenical reading of the regime that launched the established church. Its appeals to conscience have been read as undercutting Foxe's use of conscience as the badge of Protestants. *Monta* 283.

Thomas More's rise to the chancellorship is merely mentioned in *All Is True*. His absence here is counterbalanced by an earlier play, *Sir Thomas More*, to which it is believed that Shakespeare contributed. In a single scene thought to be written in Shakespeare's own hand, *Greenblatt* 263, Thomas More is seen as sheriff of London quelling a riot. The rioters are citizens outraged by the oppression of foreigners, "the Lombards," who rely on royal patronage. More reminds the citizens of their duty to obey the king, the representative of God. He then asks them to consider how they would like to be treated if they were foreigners. His second argument recalls Isabella's to Angelo, in *Measure for Measure*. It is a winning argument. The crowd declares:

Faith 'a says true; let's do as we may be done by.

Sir Thomas More, 2:4

Shakespeare's scene was probably composed in 1603-1604. *Taylor* in *Hill-Howard* 123-126. The play itself is not known to have been performed before 2005 when the Royal Shakespeare Company put it on. John Fisher, the bishop of Rochester, is also a character. The recollection of two men who became Catholic martyrs may have been too much for the Elizabethan censors. But the reasons why the play languished four hundred years are speculative. What is clear is that at the height of his powers, Shakespeare made a small and simple tribute to the memory of More.

A different view of Shakespeare's contribution is taken by David Womersley, who sees the original play by Anthony Munday as a presentation of More as one of the Reformed and Shakespeare's added scene as a speech for law and order. *Womersley*, p.305. He also dates the revision to 1594. His interpretation significantly reduces any religious implications of Shakespeare's collaboration.

A fourth play whose structure is significant is *Hamlet*, which incorporates identifiable Catholic beliefs on penance, prayer, and purgatory, beliefs which are woven together to make the coherent framework of the play. In 1600-1601, to follow *Greenblatt* 298, Shakespeare was at work on the play, keeping in mind the death of his own son Hammet in 1596 and probably aware that his own father was close to death. *Id*. 311.

Hamlet's father, as his ghost declares, died "unhouseled," "disappointed" and "unanealed." *Hamlet* 1.5.77. He speaks the language of the sacraments. "Houseled," an obsolete term, sounds like a synonym for initiation into a fraternity. To be houseled, however, is to have received the Eucharist, as in Southwell's *Corpus Christi* hymn:

> None takes him doth devide him,
>
> Receiv'd he whole perserverth
>
> Be there one or thousandes housled
>
> One as much as all received
>
> > "St. Thomas of Aquinas Hymne read on
> >
> > Corpus Christi daye," *St. Robert* 22.

The term can be used more specifically as meaning to have received the sacrament as part of the viaticum, as one sets out for the journey after death. OED. at "housel". To be annealed is to be healed by absolution. As expressed in *Jacob's Well*, a fifteenth century book in the vernacular intended for the laity, the good man was "Houselyd, anelyd, and dyed." O.E.D. at "housel." To be neither houseled nor healed is to be in a perilous state; "disappointed," now obsolete in this sense, is to be unprepared. Hamlet's unprepared father is placed in purgatory, not named but identified, as "my prison-house" in which sins are "burnt and purged away." *Hamlet* 1.5.12-13.

As his father's ghost moves about, Hamlet exclaims, *"Hic et ubique." Hamlet* 1.5.158: "here and wherever." The phase is from the post-Tridentine *Missale Romanum*, (p.139), Under the general heading *Orationes diversae pro defunctis* and the specific heading *Pro his qui in cemeterio requiescent*, there follow three prayers in which the phrase is used.

The first prayer asks God grant pardon for their sins to his male and female servants *"et omnibus hic et ubique in Christo quiescentibus"* [= "and to all here and wherever resting in Christ"]

The second prayer, under the subhead *Secreta*, offers the host to God for the souls of his servants *"et ominium catholicorum hic et ubique in Christo dormientium"* [= "and of all Catholics here and wherever sleeping in Christ"]. that this *sacrificum singulare* free them from "the chains of dreadful death."

The third prayer, under *Postcommunio*, asks that to his servants *"quorum corpora hic et ubique in Christo requiescent"* [= "and whose bodies here and wherever rest in Christ"]. God grant coolness, a blessed quiet , and a clear light.

Whichever of the three prayers Hamlet alludes to, he is referring
to souls who are not damned. It is hard to see *hic et ubique* being part of
Hamlet's education. It must have been part of Shakespeare's.

The prison house of the ghost is again noted when on its departure
Horatio salutes the cleansing coming of day:

> The cock that is the trumpet to the morn
>
> ... , at his warning
>
> . . .
>
> The extravagant and erring spirit hies
> To his confine
>
> *Hamlet* 1, 1, 148-156

Horatio is paraphrasing in English the hymn written by
St. Ambrose and used in the liturgy for Lauds on Sunday:

> Praeco diei iam sonat
>
> . . .
>
> Hoc omnis erronum cohors
> Viam nocendi deserit.

In English   Now the herald sounds the day

> . . .
>
> This whole band of lawless vagabonds,
> Forsakes their path of evil-doing.
>
> *Devlin* 1963 31

Such echoes of the liturgy seem to arise from the poet's own store
of memory.

Hamlet does not doubt what destiny provides for the good man as
he advises Horatio:

> Absent thee from felicity awhile.
>
> *Hamlet* 5.2.19.

At the very end of the play, the concern with a good death recurs in the prayer of Horatio:

> Good night, sweet prince,
>
> And flights of angels sing thee to thy rest.
>
> *Hamlet* 5.2.302-303.

In this single sentence, Shakespeare paraphrased the Latin prayer said or hymned on the way to the grave:

In paradisum deducant te Angeli; in tuo adventu accipiant te. Martyres et perducant te in civitatem sanctam Jerusalem. Chorus Angelorum te suscipiat, et cum Lazaro quondam paupere aeternam habeas requiem.

In English:

May the angels lead you into paradise. At your coming may the martyrs receive you and bring you into the holy city of Jerusalem. May the choir of angles receive you, and with Lazarus, who once was poor, may you have eternal rest.

Benedictines of the Solemnes Congregation, p.1778.

The passage had deep roots. For Christians of the patristic age, coming out of the Greco-Roman world, the voyage of the soul after death to God was long and hazardous; an angel was needed as a guide. *Graeka* 25. By 800 A.D., a prayer said at home at the instant of death was part of the viaticum or commendation of the Christian soul on its way. The prayer asked the angels and saints to meet the soul and, then, addressing the soul directly and God indirectly, prayed

> May the choir of angels welcome you and with
>
> Lazarus, once poor, may you have eternal rest.
>
> *Ritter* 43.

Already the angelic chorus and the figure of Lazarus (a blend of Luke 16:23-25 and John 11:1-12:7) are joined.

William Allen, a Lancastershireman recently ordained abroad
and eventually a cardinal and a chief mover in Rome on matters of
England, published in 1565 a substantial tract, in English, on purgatory
and prayer for the deceased. In distinction from the diminished rites
of the reformers, he set out old and universal practices at Christian
funerals– the lights, the ringing, the place of buried itself "and such
like" all intended for "the solace of the living"; hymns and psalms in
thanksgiving to almighty God; and "the principal thinges" – prayers
and sacrifices whereby the departed were "assuredly much profitted by
release of theyre paynes." *Allen* 201b-202a.

The burial service provided Hammet would probably have had a
bleak brevity. *Greenblatt* 315. It would have lacked the cadence of
the Latin, rich in its physical imagery, culminating in the song of the
angelic reception committee. The ancient prayer asks for the welcome
into heaven that Katherine sees in her vision in *All Is True*. In Horatio's
single sentence, Shakespeare has compressed the reception by the
angels and their song of welcome.

It is an anticlimax to add that, besides the echoes of the liturgy,
Hamlet uses oaths – oaths inappropriate for the student at Lutheran
Wittenberg that he is said to be, but consonant with the Catholic
culture of pre-Reformation England. He swears by St. Patrick, *Hamlet*
1.5.136; by Our Lady, *Id.* 3.2.146; and by God's blood, *Id.* 3.2.300, the
last invoking the transsubstantiated wine in the mass. These oaths are
as suggestive as the liturgical reminiscences.

Illustratively not comprehensively, suggestively not demon-
stratively, the passages in the plays just noted – *A Midsummer Night's
Dream, Measure for Measure, All Is True* and *Hamlet* – constitute
markers pointing to a path Shakespeare had walked.

Lancaster. Examples from the plays may be supplemented by
the launch of what only can be called the Lancaster hypothesis – a

speculation, intriguing, plausible and not demonstrated. It appears to have been first suggested in 1937 by Oliver Baker and picked up by E. K. Chambers in 1944. *Wymer* 272. It received attention in Alan Keen and Roger Lubbock's *The Annotator* (1954), whose principal point was that the anonymous reader who had entered marginal Catholic glosses on Hall's *Chronicle* was probably Shakespeare himself. The hypothesis took on solidity in 1985 with E.A. J. Honigmann's *Shakespeare: The Lost Years*. In the subsequent twenty-five years the hypothesis has been debated, substantially accepted by a critical biographer, Park Honan in *Shakespeare: A Life* (1998), and sympathetically if tentatively entertained by *Greenblatt* 104-108.

To summarize the evidence presented by Greenblatt, the Lancaster hypothesis supposes that Shakespeare, finishing school in Stratford at 15 or 16, was recommended by John Cottam, the Stratford schoolmaster, to Alexander Hoghton or Houghton in Lancashire, the most Catholic shire in England; Hoghton was a feudal magnate presiding over a large household. A prominent Catholic, he would have relied on the advice of Cottam, whose brother was a Jesuit.

On this hypothesis, Shakespeare would have traveled north in 1580 and become a tutor and an actor in Hoghton's entourage. In 1581, Hoghton recommends "William Shakeshaft" in his will. In Lancashire, Shakespeare would not only have encountered a more vigorous Catholic culture, he could have encountered Edmund Campion, who conducted a part of his missionary work moving from one Lancashire household to another. *Greenblatt* 109 even imagines the adolescent Shakespeare kneeling before the charismatic Jesuit. The Lancashire hypothesis is rounded out by the possibility that in Lancashire Shakespeare first made a connection with the troupe of actors licensed as Lord Strange's Men, with whom his later London career took off.

The Lancaster hypothesis remains an hypothesis, and one sharply disputed: first, because "Shakeshafte" is not "Shakespeare"; second, because Campion was in Lancaster for, at the most, two months in the spring of 1581. *McCoog and Davidson*, 181. It is hard to go beyond the kind of speculation that solves a detective story before the final chapter is reached.

Beyond speculation, Campion held a place in Shakespeare's mind. In *Twelfth Night*, the clown Feste, disguised as a clergyman, says:

Bonos dies, Sir Toby, for as the old hermit of Prague that never saw pen and ink very wittily said to a niece of King Gorboduc, That is, is

Twelfth Night 4.2,11-13.

This passage looks like harmless nonsense. It is certainly gratuitous. The Norton edition of Shakespeare with an introduction by Greenblatt glosses "the old hermit of Prague" as "probably an invented authority." But the authority is not invented. Prague was Campion's assignment before he was sent on the English mission. In 1573, he had begun his novitiate there and, after an interval at Brno, had returned to teach there until 1580. *McCoog (2007), xxvii.*

That Campion is meant is confirmed by the play on a poem entitled, "Why do I use my paper, ink and pen?" This poem, probably written by Henry Walpole, a member of Gray's Ina, was composed in honor of Campion. It was printed once, suppressed by the government, and widely circulated within the Catholic community in manuscript. *Kilroy* 59-64. Its opening verse was set to music by Byrd. *Kerman 1981*, 43. Feste's seemingly irrelevant comment is an allusion, challenging the poem's opening line. No equivocator, Feste states the simple truth, "That is, is." Even the reference to the niece of King Gorbuduc is not chance. A torturer of Campion in the Tower was Thomas Norton, the author of the play *Gorbuduc*. *Wilson* 98. In the scene in *Twelfth Night*, Feste, calling himself Persons, turns the tables on the hypocritical

Puritan, Malvolio, and makes him undergo a torment far less severe than Campion's. Feste bears nearly the name of Campion's partner, Robert Persons.

In the July 4, 2010 production of the play in Ashland, Oregon, the entire exchange was eliminated without explanation or regret. It is unintegrated in the play. The more reason, then, to think about why the playwright added it.

<u>Usual suspects</u>. The Lancashire hypothesis relates back not only to John Cottam, whose brother Thomas became a Jesuit martyr executed with Campion. Shakespeare's schoolmaster from the age of 7 to 11 was Simon Hunt. I have heard a wise judge say that these are the years where education is most significant. Hunt left England to become a priest; he became a Jesuit in 1578. *Greenblatt* 19. At least one Stratford schoolboy got Hunt's message. Shakespeare's schoolfellow, Robert Dibdale, left England, became a priest in 1584, returned as a missionary in 1585, and was captured and hung at Tyburn in 1586. *Taylor* 292; *Caraman*, "Martyrs" 325.

School teaching was the business of the established church. According to that church's canons of 1571, schoolmasters had to be licensed by the bishop, who was to act only after being assured of their character. *Bray* 201. Whether or not Shakespeare's teachers were cleared in this manner, the initiative for their appointment came from the Stratford town council. Disregarding the law, the Stratford town fathers had put their school in the charge of Cottam and Hunt, graduates of Oxford whose Catholic connections were unmistakable.

Beyond the school was the family. Mary Shakespeare, William's mother, was an Arden, a family distinguished in the county, whose name went back to the Domesday Book and graced a great expanse of woods known as the Forest of Arden. Mary's connection with the main branch was distant but valuable. The main branch and her own parents were Catholics. *Greenblatt* 59. There is no evidence that Mary altered her childhood faith.

Anne, Shakespeare's wife, came from Protestant stock. *Id*. 116. But Susanna, their daughter, placed a stone on Anne's grave in 1623 and had on it these words carved:

A mother's bosom you gave and milk and life, for such bounty, alas! I can only render stones. Rather would I pray the good angel to roll away the stone from the mouth of the tomb, that thy spirit, even as the body of Christ, should go forth. *Greenblatt* 325.

This inscription is a public prayer. It is not meant literally as though Anne Shakespeare's spirit inhabited the grave. It is addressed, contrary to the established church, to a soul who can hear her prayer. The direct addressee is her mother, as Horatio's prayer is addressed to the soul of Hamlet. The indirect addressee is God who alone can answer the prayer to release a soul from purgatory.

Susanna carried the name of the comely and courageous heroine celebrated in the Book of Daniel in the Latin Vulgate. The book was eliminated by the reformers as apocryphal. The play of *Edward III*, at least in part by Shakespeare, commemorated the intrepid Israelite. *Sams* 163-164. Bearing the biblical name and married to a Protestant, Shakespeare's daughter was listed among those refusing to receive communion at her parish church as the legislation enforced after the Gunpowder Plot required. Subsequently she was one of seven ignoring a summons to appear in court. The case was not prosecuted to a conclusion. The evidence that in 1606 Susanna was a recusant is strong. *Hanley* 441. The evidence that Susanna was her father's favorite is equally strong. He made her his principal heir. *Greenblatt* 244. In this respect, his will is, as *Greenblatt* 389 observes, "a remarkable declaration of love."

John, Shakespeare's father, was an officer required to supervise the alteration of the Catholic church in Stratford. Scenes on the walls of the church depicted the saints. Their removal was part of the process of alteration. Whitewashing them was effective in removing them from view. Whitewash was applied in Stratford. But the removal could be read as temporary. Whitewashing could be preservation for the future. An official report made in the 1580's notes that "in an hour" a whitewash may be undone. *Duffy* 583. The ambiguity of the act makes assessment of John Shakespeare's beliefs uncertain. As a councilman, he would have had a hand in hiring the Catholic schoolmasters. *Greenblatt* 95-96. He was listed in 1591 for not attending divine service. Was it because he feared a debt collector or was he a recusant? The evidence is unclear. *Id.* 62.

Sometimes urged as evidence of his beliefs is a document styled "Spiritual Testament." The "Spiritual Testament" was a formulary of prayers composed in Milan under the auspices of its archbishop, Carlo Borromeo, circulated in printed form, and translated from the original Italian into the vernacular of the country where it was used. It has been argued that nothing shows the formulary to have been in use in England in the late sixteenth century, but the hypothesis has been advanced that it formed part of the missionary supplies brought with them by Persons and Campion in 1580; they had stayed in Milan with Borromeo en route. In 1581, William Allen wrote Alfonso Agazzari, "Father Robert asks for three or four thousand or even more of the English Testaments, for they are desired by many." The letter suggests that Robert Persons is distributing the spiritual testament widely. The counter suggestion is made that Allen is referring to the Douai translation of the New Testament. This possibility, however, is controverted by another letter of Allen to Agazzari speaking of sending "two or three testaments," which "are larger than our foot-messengers about to depart can carry."

In this letter the newly-translated New Testament must be meant. If two or three were too much to carry on foot, Persons could scarcely have sought three or four thousand for England; he must have been asking for the Spiritual Testament which consisted in a handful of pages. *Takenaka* 18-19. The form, with blank spaces for the name of the person using it, and the name of that person's patron saint could have reached England in John Shakespeare's lifetime.

John Shakespeare's name was filled into the appropriate blanks of a Spiritual Testament, with St. Winifred filled in as his patron. A manuscript marked in this way was transcribed and printed in 1790 by Edmund Malone, in an addition to his edition of the works of the playwright. The manuscript itself has now been lost or destroyed. If John Shakespeare were the spiritual testator, it would establish his beliefs and be marginally relevant to his son's. The circumstances of the document's eighteenth century discovery, coupled with ignorance of how and when John Shakespeare would have been led to sign it, have put the case for its authenticity in doubt. *Bearman* 184-202. At most, its authenticity is no better than plausible. *Greenblatt* 317. Like the evidence for the Lancaster hypothesis, it provides plenty to stimulate speculation.

The Spiritual Testament establishes nothing as to William Shakespeare's faith. What it does do is to show the kind of Catholicism being imported from the continent by the missionaries. It is a baroque creation, extravagant in the self-abasement of the sinner who makes the document his own and in its arsenal of anxious prayers to be preserved in grace. It is testimony not to what William Shakespeare believed but to a continental current with which he was likely acquainted.

Add three bits of hearsay by writers, two of whom did not know Shakespeare personally, but who had no obvious motive to impute Catholicism to him: The Protestant historian John Speed, writing in 1611 while Shakespeare was alive, referred to "this papist and his poet, of like conscience for lies, the one ever faining and the other ever falsifying the Truth"; the reference is believed to be to Robert Persons and Shakespeare. *Taylor* 296. If well-informed, Speed meant not Persons but Southwell. Richard Davies, sometime Anglican chaplain of Corpus Christi College, Oxford, declared – long after Shakespeare's death – "he died a papist." *Id.* Davies may reflect a sense that the poet "had returned at the end of his life to the point from which he had begun." *Greenblatt* 387. Davies' statement comes too late to count as evidence. Speed's surly remark could be discounted as malicious gossip. In the mouth of Speed, it is an accusation of Shakespeare, if Shakespeare is meant.

What is not a speculation by someone who did not know him but is a smear or a sneer by someone who did comes from Robert Greene. In the first notice of Shakespeare by the coterie of playwrights he encountered in London, Shakespeare himself is described as a crow. He was in Robert Greene's biting phrase "an upstart Crow, beautified with our feathers." *Greenblatt* 213. Greene was a graduate of Cambridge who had led a dissolute life in London, the companion of "cardsharps, forgers, and pickpockets." *Id.* 205. His comments on Shakespeare, published posthumously in 1593, reflected his envy of the new man's success and "had something of the finality of a curse." *Id.* 213. His carefully chosen words must have hurt. Shakespeare was an upstart: he was not a university graduate. Why was he a crow? It was not because he cawed. As will be more fully developed apropos of Sonnet 70, a crow in popular parlance was a Jesuit. Greene maliciously chose a term that would identify Shakespeare with the Catholic ultras: in his hyperbole he was a Jesuit. In the same postmortem blast at his rivals, Greene marked Christopher Marlowe as an atheist. *Id.* 212. Something in each of his two rivals was seized on by Greene and then pushed hard. Shakespeare was set down in a religion that the new man did not advertise. Greene's choice of bird for Shakespeare is not random.

Greene is, of course, open to challenge as a witness to Shakespeare's faith. When Greene called Marlowe an atheist, was he really one or was Greene indulging in defamation of a rival? Does Greene know what Shakespeare believes or merely pass on speculation that is meant to be unpleasant. We cannot be sure. The economy and malice of the comment catch our attention as they would have caught the attention of any reader of the time.

Putting together his background, the gossip, and the plays, what can be concluded? Some of the evidence is consistent with the author being a devout Anglican. A George Herbert or the John Donne of the *Holy Sonnets*, for example, could have felt the pressure of the paradox of redemption explored in *Measure for Measure*. Other evidence marks the man a little differently. In the plays the old hermit of Prague and the mermaid on the dolphin's back unobtrusively introduce Catholics martyrs. In her vision Katherine of Aragon is treated as another candidate for such veneration. Latin lauds are paraphrased and a Latin burial hymn compressed in *Hamlet*, whose plot hangs on the existence of Purgatory. Hyperbole, always active in Shakespeare, is uncontrolled in *Titus Andronicus* as if a consciousness raw from seeing contemporary barbarities committed by authority could not control a wounded outburst. A Catholic consciousness would account for all these things. Is the proof in the plays? Yes, but not conclusively.

None of the scattered pieces are decisive, none is a zero. The evidence adds up, so that by the twenty-first century, Jeffrey Knapp can conclude, "Shakespeare in all likelihood was raised a Catholic," *Knapp* 50, and Gary Taylor can suppose him to have been one throughout his life. Scholarship on Shakespeare's religion incorporates judgments impossible in any century before the present. The way is open to an hypothesis linking what is known to the poetry I call spiritual.

A capital qualification: any guess as to Shakespeare's religion must allow for inconsistency and change in his beliefs. If the thesis advanced here as to the Spiritual Sonnets is true, they are themselves testimony to such change. At one time, as Sonnet 117 puts it, the poet "sailed to all the winds." No basis exists for classifying Shakespeare all his life as a devout Christian or as a crypto-Catholic. For our purposes, what is relevant are the beliefs he held when he wrote the Spiritual Sonnets.

A Wayfarer on a Christian Way: An Hypothesis. We are chiefly interested in his opus not Shakespeare's life. Yet the two cannot be easily disjoined. What he believed as a man at the time he wrote shaped what he wrote. We do not know what his words meant unless we have a sense of how he meant them. To conclude with Taylor that in the plays Shakespeare created "a secular commodity" is to attribute to him the stance of a playwright of the twenty-first century.

It is possible, I think, to put together the pointers to the poet as a believing Christian and tentatively and hypothetically sketch Shakespeare's central convictions when he composed the sonnets considered here. What follows in this book on the specifically spiritual poetry of Shakespeare conforms with this hypothesis and will confirm it not by a Euclidean demonstration but by a convergence of probabilities.

Harry Levin, the most judicious of critics, has written: "Shakespeare was indubitably a Christian, ethically and culturally speaking, insofar as Christendom had shaped his frame of reference." *Levin* 98. But Levin goes on to say that the religious warfare of the times had left "the alert and sensitive spectator to be impressed by the very clashing of creeds." No doubt. The revolution of the times enlarged the poet's mind beyond the conventional categories. Should we then see Shakespeare as a spectator, a man without his own commitments? Robert Greene, who had so little use for him, made one acute observation as to his character. Shakespeare, Greene declared, had "a tiger's heart wrapped in a Player's hide." *Greenblatt* 213.

Greene's line was a take-off of a line of Shakespeare's:

O tiger's heart wrapped in a woman's hide

3 *Henry VI* 1.4.138.

Spoken by York in bitter reproach to Queen Margaret, the line is not a compliment. In Greene, it is partly parody but parody with a grain of truth. Greene did not imagine that Shakespeare was a neutral, above the clash of creeds.

Receiving the Shakespeare Prize at Hamburg University, Graham Greene took the occasion to contrast Southwell's bold defense of his religion with Shakespeare's silence in the plays; Shakespeare exchanged his "prudent tongue for the friendships at Court and the great house at Stratford." In his subsequent reprint of his speech, Greene repeated his dislike of "something cold and prudent in the poet's nature." *Greene 1972*, p.2.

It is not for anyone who does not face the manacles, the rack, the hurdle, and the gibbet to disparage one who risked them all but tread with prudence to speak the truth and celebrate the martyred. He ran no great risks, Graham Greene might reply. Everyone at court knew that William Byrd and Countess Arundell were Catholics and nothing bad happened to them. In that small society in which everyone knew everyone else and let a good deal go unnoticed, Shakespeare was in real danger of being tortured or killed only if he had been hiding a priest or actively plotting to bring down the government. But he was a moderate man, counseling his confreres against violence.

Graham Greene's possible answer underrates Shakespeare's capacity for empathy. Would a tormented tiger stay tame? Would an abused tiger merely muse in a world of metaphysical abstractions? If he had any experience of the persecution, if answers to deadly questions were forced from his friends, if betrayals were secured by bribes and led to the ruin of entire families he knew, if idealists innocent of secular misdeeds were drawn, hung, and quartered because of their priesthood and friends and relatives tortured or killed because of their hospitality to the hunted, would a tiger be still? Would he turn these real sufferings into "a secular commodity?" If the tiger were a person endowed with extraordinary empathy, would he swallow his sorrow?

In a secular society religion does not have the robust reality it possessed for people of 1600. A possible, if not plausible, reading of the religious poetry of the day is to characterize it as "political." Of course a religious position in 1600 carried with it political allegiances, opportunities and risks. A persecuted religion, however, was embraced not to enhance one's political position, which it undermined; the disfavored political stance was concomitant to the religious commitment.

A persistent presumption exists that there is only one kind of Catholic. That presumption is uppermost with old-fashioned Protestant writers and with modern secularists. It is a presumption fed by the orthodox – should I say the ultra-orthodox   within the Catholic Church who hold that any deviation, jot or tittle, from Roman rule disqualifies a believer from being a Catholic. There are and have been, in fact, several kinds of Catholics. Unless one could read their hearts – and God alone can do that – one cannot determine the vital strength of their beliefs. Even the Inquisition did not pretend to judge hearts.

Most relevantly to our present investigation, there is the critical Catholic, of whom Erasmus is the most conspicuous example in the sixteenth century. Loyal to the Church, fiercely hostile to abuses within it, willing to ask whether accepted teaching – e.g., on divorce s– was beyond revision, seeing the good the Reformers aimed at, Erasmus has often been mistaken by Protestants as a fellow-traveler, treated by secularists as an heroic rebel, and dammed by conservative Catholics as a heretic. Yet Paul III wanted to make him a cardinal. See Bene, 207-209.

Shakespeare – I shall argue from the Spiritual Sonnets – shares the spirit of Erasmus, whose *Moriae Encomium (Praise of Folly or Praise of* [Thomas] *More)* ridiculed the theologians' cheers for the persecution of heretics. The folly of these learned fools was the very opposite of the Christian folly of following Christ. As *Booth* 249 suggests, Erasmus's work may be behind the barb at "doctor-like" folly in Sonnet 66. Violence, Erasmus maintained, was not the way of repairing the harmony of the Church. See *Noonan* 2005 153.

Erasmus, Cervantes, Montaigne – these are the great humanists to whom Shakespeare invites comparison. They stand in sharp contrast to those who might polemically be termed the ultras, narrow in their notion of noxious novelty, supremely conscious of the rightness of all ecclesiastically proclaimed positions; unconscious of any flaws in the fabric they fashioned of invincible certainties; aggressively eager to assert their superiority. Such Catholics existed. Shakespeare kept a wide berth from them. To use their existence in order to deny the Catholicism of an Erasmus or a Shakespeare is a polemical position.

Shakespeare's beliefs could not have been unknown to some who could have censured him for them, but he is never indicted for them. He is familiar with the Catholic community in London and its Jesuit mentors, whom, as we shall see, he praises and cautions. "Shakespeare never sacrificed anything for anybody," a cynical pen once wrote. Can one be so sure? As we shall see, Shakespeare takes risks. He is aware that the hazards are large. He has mastered the unwritten rules by which his life and his beliefs can be kept. He is no fanatic ready to fire a train of gunpowder. He can only deplore and distance himself from such adventurism. He is no choirboy always in tune with the choir. His mind in religious matters, as in others, is attentive, observant, complex, active. His beliefs evolve. In his maturity he is a critical Catholic and, critically, he is a Catholic. He is a critical Catholic not by a sour scepticism about the spiritual sense of Scripture or the existence of any tradition or the authority of authority; but by an alert awareness of the arrogance and abuses of authority, the danger of dogmatic hatred or *odium theologicum*, the cruelty and the foolishness of religious persecution.

Unlike Southwell, Shakespeare is not a martyr. To be hunted and hung was not his vocation. Unlike Byrd, Shakespeare was not engaged in providing music for the Church of England, nor was he using his art to provide music for the mass. But like Byrd, as we shall see, he did use his art to celebrate the martyrs and to offer himself to God as though he were at mass. Like Southwell, as we shall also see, he could be the passionate celebrant of love in its largest sense.

An oppressed minority may be hardened by pressure or splintered by it and the maneuvers of the oppressors. The oppressors, less exposed to pressure, may divide in the struggle for power or over doubts as to policy. The Burghley-Essex conflict that ended in Essex's execution illustrates a power struggle; the oscillating course of the persecution of Catholics manifests uncertainty about the most efficient means of curbing, even crushing, the old religion. Only an idiot would have assumed that the oppressors were united. Shakespeare was not an idiot. Even while suffering the oppression, he could stroke one part of those in power. Beyond expediency, he may be seen as a man seeking peace.

Odium theologicum – theological hatred – is the opposite of the love fundamentally required of Christians. Perhaps because it expresses such a profound rejection of the great commandments of love, theological hatred may usually contain an element of bad faith, a sense that one is acting perversely in exalting purity of doctrine above love of one's neighbor. This dim consciousness of perversity must be strenuously suppressed and so the hatred is sharpened. For this reason, theological quarrels have been marked, on occasion, by extraordinary bitterness. The bitterness is intensified if the quarrel is within a minority trying to maintain itself in an environment that is oppressive. These reflections may suggest the currents running through and dividing the Catholic community in Elizabethan England. To survive and not fall into factionalism, fanaticism or despair required fortitude and balance of mind.

Ever since Lady Margaret, the grandmother of Henry VIII, had sponsored Caxton in printing an English translation of Thomas a Kempis, *The Imitation of Christ*, this classic work of late medieval spirituality had been a touchstone for English Catholics. In her life of Southwell, Anne Sweeney has found lines from it apposite to him, ardent missionary though he was. They fit with equal or greater force the life of William Byrd and the life of the third man between Southwell and Byrd, William Shakespeare. Byrd, Southwell, Shakespeare, each in his own way a peacemaker, could be summed up in these words from *The Imitation*:

Sed cum duris et perversis aut indisciplinatis pacifice posse vivere magna gratia est et laudabiliter nimis virileque factum.

In English:

> But to be able to live in peace with the hard and the perverse or
> the disorderly
> Is a great grace and exceedingly praiseworthy
> And a virile deed.
>
> *The Imitation of Christ* II, 2.

Preoccupied in 1601 with death and with after-death, the poet did such a deed. He composed a poem celebrating a martyr of Love.

4. Love's Marker

The obvious, David Daube used to observe, is what is not stated in a law; the lawmakers think it unnecessary. Examples are legion. Take one from academe. The statutes of St. John's College, Cambridge, said nothing about the admission of women. Founded by Lady Margaret, this college for over four centuries was a college for men; it was self-evident that women would not think of applying. In those benighted times it was assumed that references to the male gender included women: women were therefore not barred by the college statutes specifying "men." But unwritten custom prevailed over the standard grammatical construction. To bar women, legislation was not necessary. Change was effected only in 1981 by the Queen in Council explicitly stating that the gender of all pronouns included the feminine.

In a different vein, my old teacher, Jack Bate, has written of "that rarest of all things for frightened and confused human nature – the obvious." *Bate* 405. One's own mortality is the decisive example. When looking at the literature of a time not our own, we must consider what was obvious at the time and why it was not stated – because everyone knew it and needed no reminder of it or because it was the thousand-pound gorilla in the room, too uncomfortable a companion to confront.

Ever since Aesop, allegorical fable has been a way that the oppressed can voice their views of their oppressors. To do so, they must put on an animal's head or the feathers of a bird. Suitably disguised, they can say what in fact is obvious – obvious to them, obvious to the self-aware among the oppressors, and too obnoxious to all the oppressors to be stated openly.

Incontestably, the poem now to be considered is about birds, and equally incontestably, it is an allegory. The phoenix, featured as its subject, was a figure familiar in European literature. The bird was endowed with a kind of immortality. As early as Lactantius, the teacher of Constantine, the bird had been identified with Christ. Petrarch had given the symbol secular significance in the poetry of love. *Rollins 1931* ix-x. *The Phoenix Nest*, a miscellany celebrating not only human love but chastity and virginity, was registered at Stationers' Hall in 1593. *Id.* The phoenix was a personage capable of being set to a variety of uses.

In 1874, Emerson put this poem by Shakespeare, long unnoticed or uninterpreted, in a collection of poetry that he edited. Emerson noted of Shakespeare that "a universal poetry began and ended with him." He placed this poem among poetry not for the world of readers but "for bards proper." He wrote:

I should like to have the Academy of Letters propose a prize for an essay on Shakespeare's poem, "Let the Bird of Loudest Lay," and the "Threnos" with which it closes, the aim of the essay being to explain, by a historical research into the poetic myths and tendencies of the age in which it was written, the frame and allusions of the poem.

Emerson, v-vi

Sixty years later, an American woman studying at the Sorbonne, Clara Longworth de Chambrun (sister of Nicholas Longworth and sister-in-law of Alice Roosevelt Longworth), could have claimed the prize. She had the intuition that the "requiem" referred to in the poem was based on an actual martyrdom that had occurred at Tyburn in the year of the poem's publication. The victim was Anne Line. *Chambrun* 224-235. It was a guess which no one seems to have made before. The poem was one that Shakespeare had contributed in 1601 to a mysterious miscellany of poems entitled *Loves Martyr*. I modernize the spelling.

The Loves Martyr Poem

Let the bird of loudest lay,

On the sole Arabian tree,

Herald sad and trumpet be,

To whose sound chaste wings obey.

But thou, shrieking harbinger,

Foul precurrer of the fiend,

Augur of the fever's end,

To this troop come thou not near.

From this session interdict

Every fowl of tyrant wing,

Save the eagle, feather'd king:

Keep the obsequy so strict.

Let the priest in surplice white,

That defunctive music can,

Be the death-defying swan,

Lest the requiem lack his right.

And thou, treble-dated crow,

That thy sable gender mak'st

With the breath thou giv'st and tak'st,

'Mongst our mourners shalt thou go.

The poem is within the covers of a book whose title and imprint are:

Loues martyr: or, Rosalins complaint. Allegorically shadowing the truth of loue, in the constant fate of the phoenix and turtle. A poeme enterlaced with much varietie and raritie; now first translated out of the venerable Italian Torquato Caeliano, by Robert Chester. With the true legend of famous King Arthur, the last of the nine worthies, being the first essay of a new Brytish poet: collected out of diuerse authenticall records. To these are added some new compositions, of seuerall moderne writers whose names are subscribed to their seuerall workes, upon the first subiect: viz. the phoenix and turtle.

London: Imprinted by R.F. for E. B., 1601.

A separate page, following the dreary passages from "Torquato" and the euqally dull pages on the legend of Arthur, sets off the "several moderne writers" announced by the title page and now named as follows:

HEREAFTER
FOLLOW DIVERSE
Poeticall Effaies on the former Sub-
iect; viz: the Turtle and Phoenix.

Done by the beft and chiefeft of our
moderne writers, with their names subscribed to their particular workes:
newer before extant.

And (now firft) confecrated by them generally,

to the loue and merite of the true-noble Knight,

Sir John Salisburie.

Dignum laude virum Musa vetat mori.

[SEAL]

MDCI

No apparent connection exists between "the true legend of King Arthur," the asserted translation of Torquato Caeliano, and what is "done by the best and chiefest of our moderne writers." The page announcing the diverse poetical essays virtually begins a new book. The page is completed by an anchor with this motto running around its border: *Anchor spei*, in other words, "Anchor of hope." The motto chimes with the anchor as an emblem commonly associated with the virtue of hope. *Ripa* 470. The promises of God, the hope set before us, were, in Scripture's unique use of the marine image, "an ancre of the soule, both sure and steadfast." *Hebrews* 6:19. In the absence of any conflicting evidence, there is no reason to doubt three assertions made in the title page of the addendum: the poems had not existed before the collection; they carried the names of their authors; and they were dedicated to Sir John Salisbury. It could be inferred that the subject of the phoenix and the turtle was set by the compiler of the poems so there would be some unity of theme.

The dedicatee, Sir John Salisbury, was a Welshman. His brother, Thomas, was executed in 1596 for complicity in "the Babington conspiracy," accused of acting for Mary Queen of Scots; on the scaffold, Thomas proclaimed himself to be a committed Catholic. *Duncan-Jones* 99. John became head of the family and in 1595 secured favor from Elizabeth. The guess has been made that the Robert Chester who appears on the title page of *Loves Martyr* was the Robert Chester who, although not a lawyer, became a member of the Middle Temple in 1600. *Id.* 101. In June 1601, John Salisbury was knighted, and the book's second part labeled "Hereafter" salutes him as a knight. The theory is proposed that Chester, already at work on the clumsy first part, recruited the outstanding authors of the second part to celebrate the knighthood and to promote Salisbury's election to Parliament. *Id.* 107-116. These guesses may be accurate; they tell us not very much about Shakespeare's poem.

The principal protagonists in the latter portion of the miscellany were the phoenix and the turtle, a short form of turtle-dove. Shakespeare's poem was not itself titled. Some two centuries after its publication, an editor in Boston, Massachusetts gave it the name, *The Phoenix and Turtle*, by which it is now conventionally known. *Rollins* 560. Despite the convention, it seems a mistake to pigeonhole the birds with a title unchosen by the author. I'll simply call it the *Loves Martyr* poem.

Compared to a later lament for the dead, Tennyson's *In Memoriam*, this poem evokes no personal bond between the poet and the deceased. But despite its bleak statement, "Truth and beauty buried be," it does not incorporate the kind of doubt that throbs through *In Memoriam*. Elegiac as each poem is, Shakespeare begins on a defiant note ("Let the bird of loudest lay"), engages in celebration ("co-supremes of love"), expresses hyperbolically the desolation caused by the two birds' deaths, and concludes in unshaken hope with a prayer. As to the quality and character of the work, Sydney Lanier's words are apt: "For a certain far-withdrawn and heart-conquering tenderness, we have not another poem like it." *Rollins* 564. The poem is altogether extraordinary.

No one has seriously questioned Shakespear's authorship of the *Loves Martyr* poem. Donald Foster, who attempted to bring a statistical analysis to bear on what was authentically Shakespeare, used a combination of word length and sentence length to evaluate each work attributed to Shakespeare. He gave the *Loves Martyr* poem a Grade Level or GL of 8, two numbers below the level he qualified as Shakespeare's. *Vickers* 195. His methodology and consistency in using it have been roundly and justly criticized. *Id*. 189-196. Brian Vickers, a vigilant master of the statistical method, has said nothing to impugn the accuracy of the claim of Shakespeare's authorship.

Torquato Coeliano, whom Chester purported to translate at the start of the volume, appeared to be fictitious. The other contributors besides Shakespeare were real: John Marston, George Chapman, and Ben Johnson [sic], plus two concealed as *Ignoto* and *Vatum Chorus*. The book was not inscribed in the Stationers' Register as the law required. It was printed by R. F. = Richard Field, a Stratford man who had brought out Shakespeare's earlier poems, *Venus and Adonis* and *The Rape of Lucree*. *Chambrun* 237, 239. E. B., the publisher, has been identified as Edward Blount. See the *Catalogue of Early British Books*. In the early 1600's, he was known as the publisher of chiefly continental, chiefly Catholic writers. He did not engage in the profitable business of publishing homilies delivered by priests of the Church of England. What he published and did not publish suggest his sympathies. *Taylor 2003*, 248-250. Blount was later to play a major part in the creation of the Shakespeare heritage as the principal publisher in 1623 of the First Folio. The involvement of Field and Blount suggests, but does not prove, a role for Shakespeare himself in the production of this miscellany of odds and ends, nonsense and superb poetry.

Enough evidence had been produced in 1938 of Shakespeare's involvement in the publication and its possible occasion to justify further investigation. Clara Longworth de Chambrun was an intelligent woman with a good sense of proportion. She was no Baconian babbling in the night with no language but her cry. Her book was published by a good house, Charles Scribner's and Sons. Her book carried a preface by a recognized scholar of Shakespeare. G.B. Harrison, who saluted her "new and exciting ideas." The book entered Doe at Berkeley and Widener at Harvard. Without especially emphasizing it, Chambrun had made a near-monumental discovery. She had uncovered a key to Shakespeare.

No investigation of her work followed. It was greeted "with disbelief and scorn." *Duncan-Jones* 93. I first encountered it in 2005 in the second-hand corner of a bookstore in Ashland, Oregon, where my wife Mary Lee and I had gone for the Shakespeare festival. Mary Lee made the discovery.

Ignoring or ignorant of the path pointed to by Chambrun, a typical introduction to the poem, that of Nielson and Hill, spoke of Shakespeare "exercising his ingenuity" on the allegorical virtues symbolized by the two birds, and added, "If the poem has any purpose beyond this, it would appear to celebrate a marriage that was not only childless but virginal." *Nielson and Hill* 609. This limp comment was followed by the editors musing that "it may contain more than meets the eye" but "no evidence exists for establishing an historical or personal reference."

A study begun at Harvard in 1954 as a doctoral thesis, "These Dead Birds," reviewed the academic treatment of Shakespeare's poem and was itself expanded into a book in 1965. The author bravely but unsuccessfully attempted to relate Shakespeare's poem to the mish-mash in Chester's miscellany; tried to provide an identity to Chester; and brilliantly demolished earlier academic exposition of Shakespeare's poem, taking particular joy in pulverizing the book of a scholar of an earlier generation, *The Mutual Flame* of G. Wilson Knight, as "a culmination of Knight's critical work — full of innumerable distortions." *Matchett* 128-129. Matchett triumphantly ended his own exegesis with the conclusion that the phoenix was Queen Elizabeth, whose death he found to be anticipated in 1601, while the turtle was the late Earl of Essex, recently executed by order of the queen! *Id.* 134. The poem's "co-supremes of love" were an aged virgin and a dead courtier who had rebelled against her! Matchett did produce some evidence that Essex may have been in the mind of some other contributors to the miscellany, however extraordinary his claim to have found Essex to be Shakespeare's turtle.

By 1968, the post-war generation of scholars appeared baffled by the poem. Peter Dronke, writing at Cambridge, summed up their frustration: "The Phoenix was Queen Elizabeth, or Christopher Marlowe, Sir John Salisbury, or his wife or sister-in-law or daughter, Lucy Countess of Bedford or the Fair Youth of the Sonnets." These were "only a few" of "the bewildering interpretations." *Dronke* 199. But a good critic would rise above autobiographical allusions or topical references. Arming himself, instead, with classical citations, Dronke attempted to explicate the long poem at the beginning of *Loves Martyr* and link Shakespeare's to it.

Interrupted by an apparently irrelevant account of the cities of Britain and the death of King Arthur, the main poem tells the story of two phoenixes who are brought together and die together in a "pure perfect fire." *Dronke* 203. One can see the invitation to find the material for Shakespeare's poem in this that precedes it. Undoubtedly the lead poem presented the death of the phoenix as a subject. It did not determine what Shakespeare made of it.

Dronke falters when he comes to Shakespeare's text. He is led to conclude that the bird "of loudest lay" is the phoenix herself, not yet dead, conducting the other birds in her own funeral! *Id.* 208. He goes on to be puzzled by her "married chastity," and concludes that it refers to "singlemindedness toward an absolute fulfillment, one that can be found only in death." *Id*. 210. A kind of love-death is imagined. In their "mutual flame" the two birds ascend "to be made heavenly in perfect love." *Id*. 211.

Dronke's effort is heroic – explicitly invoking *Antony and Cleopatra* and silently evoking Wagner; leaving unacknowledged the dove's earlier demise and unexplained how the phoenix leads the troop yet dies; and ignoring the request in the poem's last line to pray for the two the critic places in a platonic heaven.

The exposition did not win support. The 1997 Norton edition of Shakespeare's works simply carried a note that *The Phoenix and Turtle* was "an abstruse philosophical poem." *Cohen*, p. 1992.

The scorn and disbelief that greeted Chambrun in 1938 continued to characterize the response of the Shakespearian establishment to the evidence of the identities of the principals. The scorn is embodied in the refusal to discuss or even to mention the evidence. The disbelief appears to be rooted in the conviction that the Shakespeare about whom the establishment is built could not have held the belief animating the poem. Neither scorn nor a priori disbelief are appropriate attitudes before a poem whose elucidation demands close examination of both its text and context.

In 2002, much after Chambrun, and using none of her historical references, John Klause published a study of the literary sources of Shakespeare's poem. In particular, he noted a multitude of words and images that echoed those in a Latin mass of requiem – for example, *fidelium defunctorum*, echoed in the poem's unusual "defunctive"; *fidelium turmis*, echoed in "the troop" (*turmis*) not to be threatened; and *mors stupebat*, whose verb is kept in "Property was appalled." The last example and a dozen others were taken from the *Dies irae*, the great Latin sequence sung in a requiem. Shakespeare did not copy.

His retentive and reflective spirit, it seemed, had held the Latin in mind and used it and altered it at will. The *Dies irae* consists in eighteen stanzas and a concluding prayer. So does Shakespeare's poem. The *Dies irae* is in trochaics. So is the poem. The likelihood that neither the vocabulary nor the form are accidental is clear. *Klause 2002* 216-217. In addition, Klause identified echoes of the writings of Robert Southwell, most notably *St. Peters Complaint* – for instance, the unusual term "threnes" in line 39 of Southwell's poem and the equally unusual reference to "Arabian trees" in line 481. *Id.* 220. Klause's source study showed the *Loves Martyr* poem to be saturated in Catholic sources.

Then in April 2003, entirely independently of Chambrun and Klause, in "Another turn for the Turtle," John Finnis and Patrick Martin demonstrated what a knowledgeable reader in Shakespeare's circle in 1601 would have read. Their findings were published in the *TLS*, a periodical familiar to most scholars of English literature. The *TLS* is hospitable to reader response and not adverse to letters demonstrating the errors committed by its contributors. As far as I can determine, the published reader response was favorable and no contrary blast came from the Shakespeare establishment. The mainstream maintained silence.

Stanley Wells in 2006, as already noted, kept mum. In his most recent work he continues to ignore the article. *Wells 2010*, pp. 80-82. An obscure allusion to the *TLS* article occurs in Michael Wood's *Shakespeare*, a 2003 book accompanying a BBC series on the poet. Wood declared that Shakespeare rejected Southwell's advice to write religious poetry "the only possible exception" being *The Phoenix and Turtle*, which "we now know" was about the Catholic martyr, Anne Line. *Wood* 164. Wood said not a word more and did not cite Finnis and Martin by name. Even this reference seemed intolerable to a recent reviewer of biographical books about Shakespeare.

Without citing the *TLS* article at all, the reviewer commented on Wood: "The documentation that would cinch the argument has yet to appear." *Potter* 7 — as if documents were needed to "cinch" an argument that depended on a knowledge of historical events and persons.

In 2007, editors of *The Arden Shakespeare* published a collection of his poetry except for the Sonnets. Klause's article had appeared in a collection edited by two American professors of English and entitled *In The Company of Shakespeare*. The Arden editors ignored it entirely. They acknowledged the existence of Chambrun and of Finnis and Martin only to dismiss them without any examination whatsoever of their data. The Arden editors had a single dispositive refutation: "it is highly unlikely that any poem publicly dedicated to Sir John Salisbury could express Roman Catholic sympathies since Salisbury himself was determined, for reasons that will be explained, to be recognized as a loyal and conforming subject of the queen." *Duncan-Jones* 93-94. The reasons then explained were Salisbury's desire for support in his political career.

A priori, the Arden editors are right: it is highly unlikely. But fine words butter no parsnips, and a posteriori beats a priori every time. To the contrary of the Arden editors' conclusory assumption and contrary to the indifference of other Shakespeare scholars to Finnis and Martin, I believe that the truth of their identification of the subject of the poem is demonstrable.

The Arden editors endeavor to show a connection between Shakespeare and Salisbury. They begin by saying that it is "not inherently unlikely" that Shakespeare should join "in paying tribute to a newly-ennobled Welsh gentleman." They then reel off a number of Welsh that Shakespeare might have or possibly could have met; he even, they say, "may have encountered the man himself." *Id.* 94-96.

We are left with what is not intrinsically unlikely — few biographical facts are — and a series of guesses without evidence to establish their probability.

The conclusion of the Arden editors can be doubted on three grounds, of which the first is the implausibility of their own exegesis and the lacunae left by it. For example, they opine that Shakespeare himself might be "the bird of loudest lay." *Duncan-Jones* 116. Why Shakespeare should exhort himself to sing was not explained. The priest flanked by the crow, they said, "strongly evokes" the funeral rites of the Elizabethan Church where a minister in surplice was preceded by the black-robed parish clerk. *Id.* 117. No explanation was offered of the crow's odd dating and of its ability to reproduce other crows. Maybe, they suggested, Elizabeth was the phoenix and John Salisbury the turtle. *Id.* 118. That Elizabeth was alive and that no one ever had thought of Salisbury as her lover did not seem to be a problem. Salisbury, not dead, but very much alive, was said to see "his right" flaming in Elizabeth's sight, i.e., he had been given recognition by the queen. *Id.* 119. That the flame was destructive was not considered. That the turtle was dead was unmentioned. In the end, the Arden editors conceded, the poem resisted "full understanding." It could be classified "a brain-teaser." *Id.* 129.

A second ground for doubting the Arden editors' conclusion: the assumption on which they rest is that any writer who contributed to a work in honor of Sir John Salisbury must have had his honor in mind. The assumption is a guess. The composite of diverse poetical essays collected to celebrate his career reflects the collector's desire to get the best modern authors within the covers of the collection. An add-on, the collection was clearly made in haste. The collector took what the poets offered. He naturally put a good face on their offerings. There is no evidence other than the inner title page that Shakespeare gave a fig for Salisbury. He could simply have written a poem he wanted to put in print.

Since Chester set the theme for the contributors to the second part, it may be inferred that Shakespeare started to write with the phoenix and the turtledove as the two principal birds in mind – that is, he wrote for Chester's miscellany. The motive may have been money or it may have been Salisbury's patronage. Once Shakespeare began to write, the execution of February 27 dominated his mind.

Focusing on the occasion honoring Salisbury, the Arden editors neglect the principal features of Shakespeare's poem – that it is an allegory; that its chief characters are dead; that it is a ritual commemorating the dead. What do these things have to do with the aspiring politician whose promoter organized the miscellany of verse? The disparity between the poem's content and the Arden editors' hypothesis is the third and final reason for rejecting it.

The Arden editors' position, however, has been echoed by a very recent "biography of the mind of William Shakespeare " where one reads that Shakespeare "contributed his own brilliant little vignette of the mystical marriage of the phoenix and the turtle, the Virgin Queen and her loyal courtier." *Jonathan Bate* 317. Once again the live Elizabeth is taken as the dead bird, as if it were enough that she was a virgin. Once again a live politician is found to be represented by the other dead bird. Once again two living persons never known to have been in love with each other, let alone married to each other, are supposed to be captured in a conjugal union. Once again a funeral is read as a celebration. Once again, the text is ignored.

Unable to understand the poem because of their ignorance of its references, some critics have carried out their work of criticism with cheerful bravura. What do "topical allusions" or "autobiographical scaffolding" matter? The main thing is "the inner force" of the work as a whole. Liberated from history and the context of the work, the critic may make the poem his own. See *Dronke* 199-200. In 2010, in *Shakespeare: Sex and Love*, Stanley Wells found the allegorical meaning "irrecoverable." *Id*. 80.

If an allegory has lost its referents, Dronke's despairing counsel may have to be followed. How much would be lost! Suppose the fable Nathan tells David was the sole portion of 2 Samuel 12:1-5 that survived. The fable, poignant in itself, would exist without reference to Bathsheba, Uriah or David himself, not utterly incomprehensible but immeasurably impoverished. If history will contexualize an allegory and enrich it, let's bring on the history.

The Case for Anne Line. First, the demonstration; then its significance. Finnis and Martin's essay depended, in part, on a knowledge of historical events outside the poem's frame and, in part, on an understanding of the language employed. The points of correspondence between the language and the events are several. The force of the argument is cumulative.

Begin with the fifth quatrain of the poem that reads:

And thou treble-dated crow

That thy sable gender mak'st

With the breath thou giv'st and tak'st

'Mongst our mourners shalt thou go.

Nielson and Hill 609 gloss "treble-dated" as "long-lived," implying that the crow is one hundred years old or more. They add in a footnote that crows were thought to conceive by kissing and so would engender more of their black kind.

Academic commentators have searched the classics to find a prototype of this bird – for example Pliny's *Natural History*, x:12 reported that the raven conceives "by a kind of billing at the mouth." The relevance of this research is unclear. Why should this bird be among the mourners? Why do the academic commentators think the bird to be a 100 or more years old, when the bird stands for an actual person? Why such an antiquated bird should be invited to the funeral and deserve a quatrain to himself the commentators do not explain.

Finnis and Martin 14 tell us that "crow" was a term that Shakespeare used for "Jesuit," based on the black soutane a Jesuit would wear if not in disguise. But would a Jesuit in England have gone about in one? An answer is furnished by the Jesuit John Gerard's account of his visit to a country house to present himself as a priest to a prospective convert: "Downstairs I changed into my soutane and returned completely transformed." *Gerard* 21. Similarly, in 1599, searchers looking for a priest broke into the London home where Gerard was lodged. Before they reached his room Gerard states, "[I] took off the soutane I was wearing." *Id.* 152. It may be inferred that the Jesuits' preference for this costume was generally enough known to be an easy mark of identity.

Crows in nonallegorical usage are associated by Shakespeare with kites as carrion eaters. See, for example, *Coriolanus* 4.5.2 and 3. After the Gunpowder Plot in 1606, Shakespeare appears to accept the government's claim that some Jesuits were involved. As Macbeth and his wife discuss the murder Macbeth has just committed, he declares:

> . . . the crow
>
> Makes wing to th' rooky wood
>
> *Macbeth* 3.2.50-51.

The suggestion is that a Jesuit fled to the house of one of the conspirators, Ambrose Rookwood. But "crow" could be used defiantly by those who saw its popular figurative sense to be demeaning and wanted to reverse the evaluation, as, for example, gays in America adopted "queer" as a badge of honor. See *infra* on Sonnet 70. In the *Loves Martyr* poem, "crow" is used to mean Jesuit without hostility.

Since 1588, the superior of the Jesuits in England had been Henry Garnet. He was born in 1555. *Caraman* 4. Hence a treble-dated crow. But how with his breath did he make others of his sable gender? Finnis and Martin did not spell out all the evidence which is available in Caraman's life of Garnet. Normally, noviceship in the Society was a necessary precondition to admission. Garnet had written Claudio Aquaviva, the general of the Jesuits, about John Cornelius, a priest who for ten years had wanted to become a Jesuit but whose admission had been deferred until he served as a novice on the continent; in 1594 he was executed, still not a member. Regretting the case of Cornelius, Garnet now asked for the power to admit a priest sentenced to death, and Aquaviva granted it. In 1600 John Rigby, a layman from Lancashire, was sentenced to death; he wanted to become a Jesuit but Garnet's power did not extend so far. After Rigby's death, Garnet brought his case to Aquaviva's attention and received authority in the future to admit his own servants. *Caraman* 189 and 271. Accordingly, Garnet possessed an extraordinary, if limited, ability to engender more Jesuits. In an exercise of this power, or a broad reading of it, Roger Filcock, who shared the gallows with Anne Line, was admitted to the Society of Jesus. *Caraman* "Martyrs" 328.

Garnet's prerogative was one that only a person familiar with the customs of the Jesuits and exceptions to their rules could have known and appreciated. Shakespeare shows himself to be in the inner circle. Garnet's profession, birth year, and extraordinary faculty to make more crows fit the bird of the fifth quatrain.

Why should the long-time superior of the Jesuits illegally in the country turn out for a funeral rite? For the past eight years, Anne Line

had been the person known to the Jesuits as Mrs. Martha, a sobriquet
recalling the woman who cared for the physical comfort of Jesus.
Caraman 278. The English Mrs. Martha was the manager of a London
residence where priests could find safety. She was executed at Tyburn
in the year that Shakespeare wrote his poem. Henry Garnet had given
notice of the execution to Aquaviva in Rome. *Id.* 281. No bird could
be more appropriately bidden to her requiem than the head crow in the
country.

Details of Line's life interlock further with obscure references in
the poem. She was born Anne Higham or Heigham. She came from
Dunmore, Exeter. She married Roger Line. Both were converts to
the Catholic Church, and on that account both were disinherited by
their parents. *Gerard* 82-83. Hence the appropriateness of the ninth
quatrain:

> So between them love did shine
>
> That the turtle saw his right
>
> Flaming in the Phoenix' sight.
>
> Either was the other's mine.

Roger, the turtle-dove, saw his rightful inheritance go up in smoke.
Each's only mine or treasure was the other.

Roger was imprisoned after being captured at a house mass and,
at the age of 18, in 1586 was exiled from England, never to see Anne
again. He died in 1594. *Kelly* 910. Hence they were divided:

> Hearts remote yet not asunder,
>
> Distance and no space was seen
>
> 'Twixt this turtle and his queen
>
> But in them it were a wonder.

This, the eighth quatrain, not only memorializes their separation.
It carries a pun conveying their name. What has distance and no space?
A line.

As to the Lines' marriage, Shakespeare writes:

Leaving no posterity

'Twas not their infirmity

It was married chastity

At least since St. Jerome's defense of the perpetual virginity of Mary, the Catholic interpretation of the marriage of Mary and Joseph had been that Mary was a virgin when she gave birth to Jesus and that she remained one throughout her marriage. Robert Southwell had celebrated this unusual union in his own poetry:

Wife did she live, yet Virgin did she die.

"Our ladies Spousalls,"

St Robert, p. 4.

Does Shakespeare imply, as *Nielson and Hill* 609 suggest, that a contemporary couple had taken the same course? Such conduct was possible. Virgin maids like St. Winifred were highly prized in Catholic England as exemplars and as intercessors. *Duffy* 175-177. Still, such unusual restraint would exceed the known facts.

Anne Line is memorialized in the autobiography of John Gerard, who had put her in charge of the safe house for priests in London. Gerard notes that as a widow Anne "made a vow of chastity, a virtue she practiced even in her married life." *Gerard* 86. It is plain from Gerard's account of another widow, Elizabeth Vaux, that a married woman's vow of chastity was not a vow of virginity. Of Vaux, the mother of children, Gerard wrote, "As she could not give God her virginity, she would offer him a chaste life." *Id*. 147. In context, that means that Elizabeth Vaux vowed to remain a widow. Gerard does not mean to say more of Anne Line except that, once separated from her husband, she vowed not to engage in any sexual conduct and that then, widowed, she renewed the vow.

A vow of virginity was a serious commitment, normally undertaken only with the advice and consent of the couple's spiritual advisor. Gerard records such a vow which he advised the couple to make only for a year and, then if able to observe it, to make permanent. His advisees, "gentlefolk," did advance satisfactorily to what would be renunciation of marital sex for the rest of their lives. *Id.* 48.

Shakespeare, praising Line's virtues, seizes on her chastity, known only, one would suppose, to her spiritual advisor. The poet goes on in hyperbole to celebrate her as a virgin. Unlike the maiden phoenix of *All Is True,* this phoenix is married; and unlike the fabled phoenix and the phoenix of *All Is True,* she leaves no successor assertedly because of her "married chastity."

We do have further information about Anne Line's death that illuminates the poem. She was captured on February 2, the feast of the Purification, popularly called Candlemass. A priest, Francis Page, was dressed in white, laying out the candles for blessing and distribution to a larger than usual crowd of worshipers. A commotion was heard at the door as a band of constables sent by Chief Justice John Popham broke in. Father Page fled. Anne Line was taken. *Caraman* 278.

In a manuscript entitled *Liber martyrorum* (*Book of Martyrs*) apparently written by a person familiar with some details of her trial and execution, her story continues. Confined to Newgate after her arrest, she had been reported by her jailers as too weak to attend court. Popham directed that she appear anyway, carried in by chair if that were necessary, as it was. That was February 26. That night she experienced a vision of light. On February 27, at Tyburn she distributed gifts to the poor: first, money from her purse, then bread from a loaf in her pocket, then lace from her petticoat. Her death preceded that of the two men hanged with her. *Liber martyrorum* 4, 13-14. This account of her is owed to Sir Thomas Tresham, a Northamptonshire landowner who composed a massive manuscript constituting an encyclopedia of events, issues, and persons in the Catholic community in England between 1581 and 1605. The *Liber martyrorum* forms a section of this work. *Kilroy* 21-22.

Executed with Line were Mark Barkworth, who was a Benedictine and an Oxford man, and the newly-admitted Jesuit, Roger Filcock. *Caraman, "English Martyrs".* Henry Garnet wrote to Rome of her death, with the report that he had gathered relics from her person. In his eyes, she had died for the faith. There was no greater glory. Thomas More, the first lay martyr of the sixteenth century had led the way. *Gregory* 270. "What greater preeminence is there in God's Church than to be a martyr?" Robert Southwell had asked. *Id*. 280. There was none. Martyrs ranked above doctors (i.e., eminent theologians) and virgins. *Id*. 298. As in the prayer at burial receiving the departed, the martyrs stood just below the angels. Nowhere in early modern Catholic Europe was there a more "intense martyrological sensibility" than in England. *Id*. 275.

The attraction of the *Dies irae* for anyone familiar with the funeral rites of Catholics is evident. Paradoxically insisting on the day when judgment will be universal and inescapable, the hymn is a plea for mercy from a judge who is also our redeemer. And this judge stands in contrast to the judge who sentenced Anne Line. The images and rhythm of the poem recall the hymn. The hymn increases the poem's resonances.

A few other details that mesh with the poem may be mentioned or recalled. "Beauty brag" in the next to last quatrain may be read as the echo of the *Brag* published in 1580 by Edmund Campion – "a work of great bravura." *McCoog* 2007, "Playing the Champion," 150. Anyone sensitive to the position of Catholics in England would have heard of the *Brag*. The coincidence of the noun with the verb used by Shakespeare cannot be demonstrated to be deliberate, but the coincidence is surely suggestive when "brag" is coupled to "Beauty." The latter term could serve as a stand-in for the Church "without stain or wrinkle," as Ephesians 5:27 expresses it. The quatrain is completed by the declaration that both the Church [= Beauty] and Truth [=Revealed truth] are "buried."

The second quatrain manifests toward the owl the loathing the recusant community felt for Popham:

> But thou shrieking harbinger,
>
> Foul precurrer of the fiend,
>
> Augur of the fever's end –
>
> To this troupe, come thou not near.

The same intense emotional note is struck in Sonnet 125's reference to the "suborned Informer." *Infra*, chapter 11.

Quatrain three's reference to "this session," from which fowls of tyrant wing are barred, is an implicit contrast with the Court of Sessions where Popham presided. The one exception, the eagle, Finnis and Martin have argued, is a reference to the Earl of Worcester, the highest-ranking Catholic at Elizabeth's court. In a subsequent article, the same authors showed Worcester's connection with Catholic intelligencers communicating with co-religionists on the continent. *Martin and Finnis* 27-29.

That birds are the mourners conforms with a convention of Christian art in which birds stand for souls. One bird is not named, although summoned to begin the funeral rites. Why is this bird not of a particular species, but generic? Commentators have puzzled over the question. The probable answer is: It's a pun. It's a pun on Byrd, who for three reasons is placed in the procession. He was a friend of Henry Garnet and through him must have known Anne Line. He composed music that celebrated the deaths of contemporary English martyrs. He is present as the first mourner because there was no equal to him as a composer and he was, therefore, "of loudest lay." Talk of "defunctive music!" Shakespeare's senior by more than twenty years, Byrd was a genius here acknowledged by another genius punning on his name.

One further point from outside the poem: Anne Line's body was thrown into a common grave and was disinterred by her friends. The countess of Arundell, the widow of the martyred Philip, sent her coach to carry it to a place where Anne could be buried with religious rites. *Kelly* 910. To one privy to this event, how appropriate a re-enactment of the obsequies in verse! The priest of Quatrain 4 is dressed in a white surplice, liturgically appropriate to the occasion. He is celebrating a "requiem"; the term, an Englishing of the Latin liturgical word for "peace," had come into usage to mean a mass for the dead. *OED* at "requiem." A pun completes the quatrain. The priest has a right to celebrate the mass. If he does not do so, the occasion will lack his rite.

With the independence often exhibited by him in treating tradition, Shakespeare does not explicitly emphasize the immortality of the phoenix. The quasi-immortal bird does appear explicitly in *All Is True*. In Shakespeare's poem, the focus shifts to Truth and Beauty, buried as if they were dead.

But, no, Anne and Roger, who believed in the truth and beauty of the Church, are celebrated by the poet. They are acknowledged:

Co-supremes and stars of love

Exalted in this way because of the fidelity of their remarkable marriage or because of what they suffered for love of God, or for both reasons, they are saluted as themselves examples of incandescent love.

The Book of Common Prayer had, in 1552, dropped prayers for the dead as pointless. *Klause* 217-218. Souls were either in heaven or hell. The Thirty-Nine Articles set out to govern the Church of England under Elizabeth were approved by Convocation in 1563, then revised and approved by the queen. Article XXII was headed "Of Purgatory" and declared:

The Romish doctrine concerning Purgatory, Pardons, worshipping and adoration as well of Images as of Relics, and also Invocation of Saints, is a fond thing vainly invented, and grounded upon no warranty of Scripture; but rather repugnant to the word of God.

The Thirty-Nine Articles 14.

This article did not explicitly ban private prayer for the dead; it deprived such prayer of an object. The article also struck in passing at the invocation of the saints. Definitively, the article abolished Purgatory. Shakespeare ends the Lines' requiem:

For these dead birds sigh a prayer.

The central identifications of the Lines and of Garnet, the congruence and cumulative effect of the supporting detail, make the case that Shakespeare was celebrating a true martyr, one who died for the sake of the God who, as Scripture states:

is love and he that abideth in love, abideth in God,

and God in him. 1 John 4.16.

Like Horatio in *Hamlet* and his own daughter Susanna in life, the poet believes in prayer for the dead to the God of love. No poem in Chester's miscellany of verse better suits the title the volume bears. Anne Line is Loves Martyr.

Shakespeare, T.S. Eliot has written, "would not have found much in common with his contemporary, St. Theresa." *Eliot* 119. This comment ignores the common ground they might have shared in honoring Anne Line. In Shakespeare's world, Graham Greene once wrote, "the martyrs are quite silent." *Greene*, p.x. Anne Line, indeed, is given no lines. She is celebrated in such a way that her life surpasses that of ordinary mortals. In Greenblatt's estimation, "the fierce self-immolating embrace of an idea or an institution" is the kind of heroism that makes a saint, and it is absent from Shakespeare. *Greenblatt* 110. But Anne Line was engaged in self-immolating work, of great danger to herself and others. Shakespeare was willing to risk the dangerous repercussions of celebrating her self-immolating service.

And my poor fool is hanged.

King Lear 5.3.304 (Q Text)

Cordelia is "my poor fool." Why does her father call her a fool? Is he comparing her with his old jester? Or does the phrase chime with a phrase in Sonnet 124 where "the fools of time" are those who "die for innocence"?

As everyone knows, Shakespeare is an afficionado not only of the pun but of the play on words that an association of sounds or verbal shapes or spellings may suggest. Sometimes his word play is a stretch. Does the expositor of Shakespeare undermine his own credibility by pointing to the words in play? Where the verbal echo is elusive, its existence obviously can't form part of an argument in support of an analysis. But to be mute about the allusion or association would impoverish the exposition.

Death by hanging recalls the martyrs referenced in Sonnet 124 and it reinforces the resemblance of Anne Line's death in Cordelia's. Cordelia's hanging is not a public execution but meant to be passed off as a suicide. It is a guess whether or not the mode of Anne Line's death echoed in the playwright's mind. Cordelia's hanging is twice noted in the F text of *Lear* 5.3.232 and 274, while Q makes it the final cry of despair by Lear. Cordelia like Anne Line had done her silent stubborn duty and paid for it.

Cordelia, of course, is not Anne Line, who is an extraordinary heroine for Shakespeare. She is not a princess like Cordelia. She is no Beatrice matching wits with Benedict. She is no Rosalind turning hearts in the Forest of Arden. She is no Cleopatra, the playmate of a ruler of Rome. She is not a saint cut in a medieval mold like Marina in *Pevicles* or Hermione in *The Winter's Tale* – saints whose nobility in suffering puts them a bit beyond human comprehension; nor is she a saint like Isabella whose redeeming act of forgiving the putative murderer of her brother wins the Duke's pardon and Angelo's redemption. Nor is Anne a saint like Helen in *All's Well*, whose virtues recall Southwell's account of the citizens of heaven. *Klause 2008*, 219. Helen bears the name of the saint who found the Cross, and she expiates her early presumptiveness by penance so

That barefort trod I the cold ground upon.

All's Well 3.4.6

Saints can sin and be forgiven, so Shakespeare must have supposed. But Anne Line is not a saint restored by repentance of sin, nor is her redeeming act rewarded by another's redemption, nor is she moved into medieval hagiography. She is a real person with a husband, a married life, and friends who attend her obsequies. Unlike Shakespeare's fictional saints, she is not to be rewarded by a ruler on this earth. She is dead.

Martyrdom, as it was known to English Catholics at the start of the sixteenth century, had a legendary cast. It was what outstanding Christians had suffered under pagan Roman emperors, not something that might happen to the woman next door. When it did happen, the grim and grimy actuality came home to those who knew the martyr. To transmute a dirty death into glory is the work of the believing poet.

Line is Mrs. Martha, nicknamed in memory of the devoted, unglamourous figure in Scripture. She is the keeper of a boardinghouse. In dramatic terms, she is little more than a drudge. Shakespeare has made her a co-supreme of love. She has been transfigured by her martyrdom.

All of the above makes clear why I believe that the Arden editors' a priori is mistaken. I will recapitulate what they leave without satisfactory explanation:

> The echo of the form, rhythm, and vocabulary of the *Dies irae*
>
> The bird of loudest lay
>
> The shrieking harbinger
>
> The session
>
> The priest in surplice white
>
> The requiem
>
> The need for the priest's right (= rite)
>
> The crow
>
> The crow's dating
>
> The crow's power to reproduce by his breath
>
> The fact that both birds are dead
>
> The connection between them, expressed in a pun on their name
>
> Their intense mutual love
>
> The destruction of the turtle's right
>
> The birds' married chastity
>
> Their status as co-supremes
>
> The destruction and burial of beauty
>
> The destruction and burial of truth
>
> The reference to "brag"
>
> The request for a prayer for the two

Attempts to fit these images, lines, allusions, and laments into the life or world of Sir John Salisbury or the life or world of Queen Elizabeth wholly fail. Shakespeare could not have written this poem with queen or knight in mind. Add finally that the grave sorrow, the great reverence, the prayerful celebration that course through the poem owe nothing to the lives of the aged queen or the aspiring politician. Shakespeare's lines speak of the very recent martyr.

Sequella. The Jesuits preserved Anne Line's memory. In 1929,
she was beatified by Pius XI as one of forty English and Welsh
martyrs. On October 25, 1970, these martyrs were recognized as
saints by Paul VI in the ecumenical presence of representatives of
the British government and the Archbishop of Canterbury. *AAS* 62,
747. The greatest human capacity, the pope affirmed, is "the capacity
to love," and martyrdom was "the expression and most sublime
sign of that love." *Id*. 62, 748-749. A decretal letter, confirming
the canonization, was published the following year, noting that the
martyrs had been killed between 1535 and 1579. *Id*. 64, 257. No one in
Rome noticed that the cut-off was twenty-two years earlier than Anne
Line's death; she was the last martyr to be mentioned as if she were
an afterthought. It did not matter. She stood enrolled with Margaret
Pole (Cardinal Pole's mother), Margaret Clitherow who was pressed
to death because she would not plead to the indictment, and Margaret
Ward, a servant girl, and together with Edmund Campion, Robert
Southwell, Robert Debdale (Shakespeare's schoolmate), Philip
Howard (earl of Arundell), and the 32 others. The feast day of St.
Anne Line was set for February 27, the anniversary of her hanging.
Fitzherbert 594.

The pope prayed that the prayers of the forty now proclaimed
as saints would heal "the fearful wound" in the Church of Christ.
AAS 62, 753. Anne Line had traveled from a criminal's death, to
celebration by England's foremost poet in verse too veiled for the
subject to be discerned by most, to the status of a saint invoked to
unite the churches.

Canonized, she was commemorated internationally. A window in
Corpus Christi Church, 525 West 121st Street in Manhattan, the parish
church of Catholics at Columbia, carried a representation of her. In

April, 2005, a homily celebrated her story and Shakespeare's poem in her honor. *Wizeman* 1.

Anne Line's story at its climax is not one to reopen ancient wounds or to revive old enmities. It is the story of the triumph of love. It is in that spirit that I turn to the spiritual sonnets that the author of the *Loves Martyr* poem wrote.

5. Addressees of the Twenty-two

Sometimes a sonnet is selected as appropriate to a specific occasion. For example, in Tobias Wolff's *Old School* the narrator uses Sonnet 29 "When in disgrace with fortune and men's eyes" to provide the heading for a chapter on his expulsion from school for plagiarism. Another example of the endless quarry the Sonnets offer: the title of the poetry collection "My Saucy Boat" of the daughter in Ian McKewen's *Saturday*, is a title cleverly appropriated from Sonnet 80 "O how I faint when I of you do write." In the same way, at my father's funeral my brother Jim, a Boston lawyer, speaking in tribute to him, chose Sonnet 18 "Shall I compare thee to a summer's day." In the same way, officiating at a wedding, I, at the request of the bride and groom, read Sonnet 116 "Let me not to the marriage of true minds."

A different kind of literary appropriation is made by Louis Auchincloss's short story, "They That Have Power To Hurt." The title of the tale is the first line of Sonnet 94. In the story, the narrator, a strikingly smug or self-possessed young man, has an affair with an older married woman. Their weekly liaisons are interrupted by her travels, and the narrator effortlessly falls into a homosexual relation, disrupted by the return of his mistress. When she realizes that he's been unfaithful to her with a man she breaks off the affair; eventually she and the narrator accept each other as friends. She sends him the

Sonnets as a Christmas gift, underlining the opening octet of Sonnet 94. But the narrator thinks her "last word" is the sonnet's concluding couplet on the smell of festering lilies. *Auchincloss* 404-405.

This fictional exegesis follows the dominant view that Sonnet 94 is somehow a love poem, albeit an ironic one once its last two lines are taken into account. I shall argue below in a chapter devoted to Sonnets 69, 70 and 94 that the dominant view is mistaken. But no law forbids a modern storyteller from shaping the sonnet to his own purposes.

On November 12, 2010, Sonnet 129 was set to music and sung by Rufus Wainwright as commissioned by the San Francisco Symphony Orchestra. In this musical form, the sonnet did not strike a somber or repentant note, but appeared at least to this listener, as jaunty, defying the consequences of passionate promiscuity. Taken in isolation from context and author, this interpretation is hard to refute.

Analogously, on a larger scale, a contextless interpretation of the poems finds a spiritual, even biblical message in every one of the 154 sonnets. See *Zinman* 1-148. Once time, place and the author's intent are eliminated as irrelevant, the sonnets become plastic, useful to the purpose of any modern user.

In most of the instances I've noted, a sonnet has been yanked from the whole and treated as a poem in isolation from its larger poetic context. Unlike the objectionable practice of quoting single lines from plays out of context, this practice may be defended as not pernicious but benevolent. When we engage in this activity, we do not invoke the authority of the author, but the immediate authority of the text, isolated from its own time, place, and originator. We are free to quarry for quotable sonnets, investing them with our own meanings. Self-sufficient, each isolated sonnet stands without our need of knowing to whom it was addressed. What should not be done is to pretend that our meaning is what the poet had in mind. To determine that here one must attempt to ascertain the addressees of the Twenty-two, the poems selected for analysis here. To try to discover them we may start with the publication of the whole sonnet sequence.

The Poet, the Publisher, the Promoters. The sonnet sequence was published in 1609 under this title:

SHAKE – SPEARES

Sonnets

Never before Imprinted

It has been thought unlikely that the poet himself chose the title; but, like many authors, before and since, he could have acquiesced in the publisher's decision. The title page of each example of the edition of 1609 indicates the several participants in the production of this slim quarto: the author, identified simply by his last name, prominently featured; the printer, G. Eld; and the publisher, "T. T.". "G. Eld" was George Eld, a well-established London printer. "T. T." stood for Thomas Thorpe, "a quality publisher." He registered the book with the Stationers' Company on May 20, 1609 to secure his copyright. Neither Thorpe nor Eld are easily seen as pirates of another man's work. *Kerrigan* 427. The name of a bookseller also appears on each copy. Several different booksellers had subscribed to the publication. Of the two copies at the Huntington, for example, one's title page carries the name of William Apley, Church Court; the other's title page carries the name of John Wright "dwelling at Christ Church gate."

The first name of the author is nowhere given. These are simply "Shake-speares Sonnets." The omission suggests that the author had no part in the printing. Apart from the selection of Richard Field as his first publisher, there is no evidence that Shakespeare picked his publishers. *Murphy* 16. The combination of a publisher, a printer, and several booksellers shows how seriously the publication was meant to be a commercial success. Could the author have been left out?

In the seventeenth century editions of Donne's *Holy Sonnets* the number and sequence of the poems vary with the publisher. Donne was dead when these Sonnets were published. Shakespeare was alive. But it seems unlikely that he would have allowed Sonnet 125 to be published with parentheses where lines of poetry should have appeared. It also seems that if the Dean of St. Paul's did not seek to have his sacred sonnets published, a successful playwright might have had even less incentive or desire to see all his sonnets, profane and sacred, out before the public.

Bob Giroux, lover of Shakespeare and experienced publisher, quotes Auden's opinion that Shakespeare would have been "horrified" by the publication of this private poetry. *Giroux* 12. No way exists to test the truth of this reasonable speculation or to resolve the question of whether the order in which the sonnets stand reflects the author's intention. There is no evidence that all of the Sonnets were printed from a single manuscript. On the whole, it seems to me probable that Shakespeare did not arrange for publication of the sonnets, and that he certainly did not supervise the printing of them. The capitalization, italicization and punctuation cannot be relied on as his; at most they represent the printer's reading – not a totally insignificant guide but not decisive. In the same way, the order of the sonnets may follow that of a single manuscript or be a combination of manuscripts. The sequence of the Sonnets is not totally arbitrary; the publisher was intelligent; but the sequence cannot be assumed to be Shakespeare's.

I have generally followed the capitalization of 1609. It is occasionally indefensible but at times it may be significant. I have also kept the italics of 1609. They are deliberate and significant. In general, I've kept the punctuation, too. I have modernized the spelling.

The case has been made that Sonnet 107 "Not mine own fears nor the prophetic soul" refers to the death of Queen Elizabeth in

1603 and the situation following it. *Giroux* 192-198. Some critics, including Booth, are unconvinced. *Booth* 342-343. Accepting 1603 as one established date, and accepting the first seventeen Sonnets as related to Southampton's bachelor status, see *infra*, one can conclude that the Sonnets were written over the course of at least twelve years. The objection is made that, as a literary fashion, sonnet-writing was a feature of the 1590's. But John Donne worked on the *Holy Sonnets* from about 1600 to after 1617, mostly between 1609 and 1614. *Stubbs* 265.

The purpose of the publication must have been to make money – certainly for the publisher and booksellers, maybe for the poet. The investors must have been disappointed. Silence greeted the publication. No contemporary remarked on the appearance of poetry of such extraordinary quality. The Sonnets were ignored in 1623 when Shakespeare's plays were collected and published. In 1640, a bastard edition was produced, inflicting "unforgivable injuries" on the 1609 text. *Kerrigan* 4-6. For the rest of the seventeenth century nothing replaced the 1609 printing.

A natural assumption is that, assembled within a single volume, the poems have a unifying theme. This assumption is the basis of the common belief that the publication memorializes two dead love affairs. The assumption of unity and the corollary drawn from it are mistaken.

Autobiography? Few copies of the 1609 edition survived. John Milton, John Dryden, and Alexander Pope may not have had opportunity to read the unaltered Sonnets in their entirety. The 1609 edition was not published again until Edmund Malone brought it out in 1781. *Murphy* 95. In 1790, *The History of English Poetry from the close of the eleventh to the commencement of the eighteenth century* by Thomas Warton, a fellow of Trinity College, Oxford, gave what he termed a "general view and character of the poetry of Queen Elisabeth's age." Shakespeare was said to have "wandered in pursuit of universal nature." *Id*. III, 499. Neither the *Loves Martyr* poem nor the Sonnets were mentioned. The Sonnets waited for critical appraisal.

That the Sonnets were autobiographical was first floated in Germany where Romanticism took root earlier than in England. One of the Schlegel brothers discovered the autobiography in 1791. *Rollins* 133. The discovery was imported to England by Wordsworth, who had drunk drafts of German inspiration and in 1808 declared that Shakespeare in the Sonnets "expresses his own feelings in his own Person." *Id*. 134. Not inquiring rigorously as to whom each sonnet was addressed, Wordworth saw the Sonnets as self-expression characteristic of the romantic poetry of his own period. The poems became a pouring out of the poet's emotional life, unconfined and undirected by the audience addressed. This unfortunate approach did not become extinct in the following two centuries.

That the Sonnets were autobiography was not accepted by everyone. In 1842, Alexander Dyce wrote:

I have long felt convinced, after repeated perusals of the Sonnets, that the greater number of them was composed in an assumed character, on different subjects, and at different times, for the amusement, and probably at the suggestion, of the author's intimate associates. Dyce, p. lxxvi.

Dyce did not develop this suggestion by specific examples. He was at some pains to deal with the sonnets addressed to "a male object," poetry which "could only surprise a reader who is unacquainted with the manners of those days" when one man might write "*amatory*" verses to another. *Ibid*. lxxiii (italics in original). Dyce neatly ended further discussion by suggestion that "the male of the poems" was imaginary, a suggestion buttressed by a passage from *Don Quixote* on the propensity of poets to imagine the objects of their love.

Dyce noted a few misguided guessers, among them George Clinton, who "as if to show that there are no bounds to the folly of a critic, maintained that Queen Elizabeth was typified by the poet's masculine friend." *Ibid.* lxxv-lxxvi. The attraction of the queen for this clumsy critic was similar to the queen's repeated appearance as the phoenix in criticism of the *Loves Martyr* poem.

Trust a poet to know another poet's poetry? It is not unreasonable to think that the special sensitivity of one artist can make him resonate to another artist's work. The prosaic person from Porlock would say, "Shakespeare created characters in his plays, why not in his sonnets? The sentiments of the one are as artificial as the other. The masks of the author are never lifted." Against this pedestrian logic, the poets give testimony: Sometimes Shakespeare wrote from his heart.

Poetic intuition alone is an insufficient guide. From Wordsworth to Wilde to Ted Hughes, English poets have read Shakespeare's heart or mind or life in the Sonnets. Far less gifted critics have put together fictional biographies, linking him to one man, taken from the Sonnets and variously identified, and to one woman, taken from the same source and also variously identified but definitely not his wife. The governing assumption of all these efforts has been that the Sonnets tell a tale. The Sonnets may have to be rearranged to have the tale make sense. With thoughtful rearrangement or merely bold speculation the story of Shakespeare the lover unfolds.

The intensity and intimacy of many of the Sonnets have convinced many readers besides the poets that at least some of them speak for Shakespeare himself. That inference seems justified when he puns on his name, Will, and equally justified when he puns on the name of his wife, Anne Hathaway, in Sonnet 145. Beyond these instances, it seems hazardous to suppose that an author capable of creating a Lear, a Hamlet, a Macbeth must be speaking for himself when he writes lines of passionate sincerity. The sonnet form tempts the reader to read the declarations as personal. Is the temptation to be always resisted? I draw distinctions.

The conventions of the age show that a sonneteer may be commissioned to compose on behalf of another. A poet may even be commissioned to express love on behalf of his principal as Viola does in *Twelfth Night*. The first seventeen of the Sonnets show Shakespeare himself in this commissioned capacity, where he appears to draw upon Erasmus's *Epistle to persuade a young gentleman to marriage*. See *Booth* 135.

Lessons in commissioned sonnetry and the line dividing it from personal poetry may be learned from *King Edward III*, a play registered in 1595, whose author is probably Shakespeare, *Sams* 161-202, or whose scenes involving the Countess of Salisbury are almost certainly by Shakespeare. *Melchiori* 15. The king, a married man, commissions a poem to the countess, also married, although not to him. The chosen poet is possessed of "a lusty and persuasive spirit." He is instructed how to write:

> Better than "beautiful," thou must begin.
>
> Devise for "fair" a fairer word than "fair".
>
> > *King Edward III* 2.1.435-436.

Hyperbole is the name of the game:

> Her beauty hath no match but my affection,
>
> Hers more than most, mine most and more than more.
>
> > *Id*. 2.1.484-485.

The commissioned poet is commanded to exaggerate. Yet a doubt remains as to the efficacy of his efforts. The king ends his instruction:

> Love cannot sound well but in lovers' tongues.
>
> Give me the pen and paper, I will write
>
> > *Id*. 2.1.535-536.

Shakespeare knows what a lusty and persuasive spirit must do to carry out his commission. He is self-conscious of the difficulty. Like Hamlet's instructions to the players, "Speak the speech, I pray you," Shakespeare is commenting on what can be expected of professionals in an art he knows. In the first seventeen sonnets he had performed a task. Are some of the later sonnets also commissioned verse? The possibility is rarely considered. The possibility, even the likelihood, cannot be excluded. No reason exists why Shakespeare, scrivener for another, stopped at seventeen. As to some, Shakespeare, speaking for himself, must have said, "Give me the pen and paper, I will write."

The poetry expressing repentance after sin is, at least arguably, specifically personal. To gain forgiveness, the principal himself must avow his fault and seek his own absolution. Redemption, in Christian perspective, comes from the saving sacrifice of Christ. That perspective is united to belief in personal responsibility. The offense has been to God. The apology and plea for mercy must be to God. Christ has died for us, but no one is saved automatically without personal repentance. Even the most debased attempts to sell indulgences for money could not promise salvation without an individual's own act of contrition. Consequently, I argue, the sonnets seeking forgiveness and reconciliation with the Church must be personal and, if personal, autobiographical.

Love objects. In 1978, in his commentary on the Sonnets, Stephen Booth shattered most speculations surrounding them. No one has engaged so closely with the text. To no one do I owe a greater debt for an understanding of the Sonnets. Booth is the best – not only the most patient, the most learned, and the most ingenious of commentators on the Sonnets, but the most representative. Other, more recent critics I quote occasionally while acknowledging that Booth still dominates the field. If I disagree with him on particular issues, as I now do, I do so mindful of his monumental work. It is for that reason that my detailed analysis of each sonnet tries to take into account what he has written about it.

Booth demonstrated conclusively, so I should think, that no one had identified the woman whom critics had come to call the Dark Lady. No one had shown that the same woman was the female figure wherever a female figure appeared. No one had demonstrated that the same man was the same addressee or the same subject in all the Sonnets involving a male figure. As to Shakespeare's sexuality, so Booth trenchantly remarked, Shakespeare was "almost certainly homosexual, bisexual, or heterosexual. The Sonnets provide no evidence on the matter." *Booth* 348.

At various times, the sexual desires manifested in the Sonnets have been a crux. In 1793, George Stevens declined to add the Sonnets to his edition of the plays because of revulsion from the Sonnets' endorsement of homosexuality. *Cohen* 1919. In contrast, a mid-twentieth century edition of Shakespeare's work by two professors at Smith College, speaks of "the fair young man" as Shakespeare's "friend" and notes "the affection of the friend" and "the favor of the friend" without further comment. *Nielson and Hill* 1409. Stephen Greenblatt, a sagacious biographer, confesses he doesn't know what went on between the poet and his patron ("stared longingly at one another or . . . went to bed together"), but characterizes the emotion expressed toward the young man as homoerotic. *Greenblatt* 253.

What we see as homoerotic could be seen by seventeenth century readers as strong male bonding. No one supposed that David had nursed a sodomitic crush on Jonathan when, lamenting his death, David declared,

> Your love for me was wonderful,
>
> Surpassing the love of woman.
>
> 2 Sam 1:26

The Bible would not have been read as endorsing a forbidden love; Elizabethans would not have read every male friendship as homosexual. Shakespeare would not have seen the love expressed for the young man as the love that dared not speak its name; the poet is scarcely silent about whom he loves.

It is predictable that some critics today will find the removal of poems they suppose addressed to the youth as deliberate dilution of the homoeroticism. They shouldn't worry. A substantial number of the sonnets remain classifiable within this genre. What is disputable is whether they all refer to the same boy. Shakespeare, it is generally acknowledged, had more than a one-track mind. The universe of his lovers or addressees could go beyond one friend and one mistress.

Booth assumed that a particular human being, male or female, was the addressee or subject of each sonnet, but was aware of allusions to religion that were not tied to a specific individual. He recognized that in Sonnet 125 "many of the particulars relate to Holy Communion." *Booth* 429. He acknowledged that in Sonnet 124 "the fools of time" might be Jesuit conspirators. *Id*. 425. He noted that in Sonnet 94 "the summer's flower" refers to virginity and is associated with those that have power, and he sees an echo of St. Paul to the Romans. *Id*. 307. He observed that Ephesians 5 "appears to have been deeply embedded in Shakespeare's consciousness." *Id*. 197. None of these glimpses of the poems' religious imagery and references moved him to think of alternative addressees.

What alternatives might there have been? Several are immediately furnished by Southwell, who wrote poetry to the Virgin Mary, to Christ, and to God. John Donne, a younger contemporary of Shakespeare, wrote his *Holy Sonnets* to God. Surely if a lesser seventeenth century poet could compose a sonnet to God, is it not conceivable that Shakespeare had anticipated him? And if Shakespeare could write a sonnet to God, could he not have written one to the Church or even to a religious order? Once the assumption is abandoned that a particular man or woman must be in view, the Sonnets are open to interpretation that is at once less confined and more stringent than that offered conventionally.

Consider again Donne's *Holy Sonnets* as presented in the Variorum edition. They were written over a substantial period of time and printed more than once. The number and the sequence vary from printing to printing. They were not designed as a single composition. Six of them were sent by the author as a gift to the "E of D," an earl who has not been indisputably identified. The *Holy Sonnets* were a series of occasional poems.

Analogously, the composition of Shakespeare's sonnets "has only a deceptive" though at times "satisfying, unity." *Edmondson and Wells* 46. Forego the satisfaction. Abandon the search for unity. Recognize the range of sentiments and the differences in addresses. Listen to the prayers. The Sonnets bring together in one sequence profane and sacred love.

The total sonnet sequence may not be intended to form a narrative. Bits of autobiography, yes. Moments of personal passion, yes. But continuous stories of desire, infatuation, love, disenchantment, no. The professional playwright is capable of putting on masks, of providing poems fitting the purposes of friends, of writing because he has been commissioned and of putting off masks and providing poems expressing his own spiritual perceptions to persons qualified to respond to them.

The first seventeen. The first seventeen sonnets leave no doubt as to the status of the one to whom they are addressed. It is a young unmarried man, who is reluctant to marry. The poems attempt to persuade him to marry and to reproduce:

But if thou live rememb'red not to be

Die single and thine image dies with thee.

Sonnet 3, lines 13-14.

The message is unmistakable. It is personally directed to its otherwise unidentified recipient urging him to a sexually reproductive union.

By resort to information outside the poems, an identification may plausibly be made: Henry Wriothesley, Earl of Southampton. The earl was the ward of Lord Burghley, who wanted him to marry Burghley's granddaughter. If the earl did not comply with his guardian's request by the age of 21, he was subject to a large fine. The earl's relatives would have contemplated this diminishment of his estate with displeasure. They, as well as Burghley himself, would have had a motive to commission Shakespeare's verses. Shakespeare formally acknowledges Southampton as his patron in his dedication to *Venus and Adonis* and more warmly dedicates *The Rape of Lucrece* to the same young nobleman, declaring "What I have done is yours, what I have to do is yours being part of all I have, devoted yours." Shakespeare would have been presumed to know what note to strike with his patron, so Southampton seems a likely candidate as the addressee, although it is not certain. *Greenblatt* 228-229. If marriage by Southampton was the poems' object, they were ineffectual but can be dated. They would have been written between 1591 and 1594, the year in which Southampton became 21, refused to marry as Burghley wished, and suffered a fine of 5,000 pounds.

A counter theory has been championed by Michael Wood and others. "Mr. W. H.", who the title page declares is "the sole begetter" of the poems, is William Herbert, later to be Earl of Pembroke. The detail that he is referred to as "Mr." is brushed aside. The young man was in need of encouragement to beget, in modern jargon, "a heir and a spare." His family was very literary; his mother was herself a poet; he later became a great patron of the arts. At a critical time in his life the family got Shakespeare to show him the way to matrimony. These sonnets would then have been written about 1597. *Wood* 179-182.

The critical 1998 edition of the writings of the Countess of Pembroke shows no trace of Shakespeare among her correspondents, guests, and patronage seekers. William Herbert was a hard case: he seduced Mary Fitton, one of the queen's maids of honor, and refused to marry her when she became pregnant. *Herbert* 18. As addressee of Sonnets 1-17, he has not gathered as many votes as Southampton. Most recently, Jonathan Bate has suggested that one batch of sonnets may be to Southampton and another, as late as 1603-1604, to Pembroke; but has then wondered if any earl would have permitted an actor such intimacy. *Jonathan Bate* 206-207.

Booth's scepticism about a specific identification has not been proved wrong. For present purposes it is enough to note that, in addition to the first seventeen, some others of the poems may well have been commissioned. They are not necessarily all from Shakespeare's heart. But I take no responsibility for reading the sonnets that have no detectable religious theme. It is no doubt true that if the Twenty-two are religious, they may cast light on the rest, and that the rest do not exist in isolation from the Twenty-two and furnish, at the very least on the printed page, their own context for them. I argue, however, that, if the contents of the Twenty-two are examined closely, their passionate engagement with those they do address is unlikely to be seen differently if poems addressed to others on other topics are brought into consideration.

<u>An introduction?</u> An argument could be advanced that Sonnet 23 should be read as an introduction to all the spiritual sonnets. It reads as follows:

Sonnet 23.
"As an unperfect actor on the stage"

As an unperfect actor on the stage,
Who with his fear is put beside his part,
Or some fierce thing replete with too much rage,
Whose strength's abundance weakens his own heart;
So I, for fear of trust, forget to say
The perfect ceremony of love's rite,
And in mine own love's strength seem to decay,
O'ercharg'd with burthen of mine own love's might.
O let my books be then the eloquence
And dumb presagers of my speaking breast,
Who plead for love, and look for recompense,
More than that tongue that more hath more express'd.
O learn to read what silent love hath writ:
To hear with eyes belongs to love's fine wit.

Two Stretches. Booth does not attempt to furnish any over-all interpretation of the poem but appears to assume that it must fall within those addressed to a young man, and he looks for sexual content. With effort he finds it in line 6. He begins by noting that "right" is an alternative spelling of "rite." *Booth* 171. He then quotes the rascal Paroles instructing Helen:

> Madam, my lord will go away tonight,
>
> A very serious business calls on him.

> The great prerogative and rite of love,
>
> Which as your due time claims, he doth acknowledge
>
> But puts it off to a compelled restraint . . .
>
> *All's Well That Ends Well* 2.4:36-39.

So glossed "the perfect ceremony of love's rite" equals sexual intercourse. Booth reinforces his argument by pointing to "a bizarre sexual undermeaning." *Id.* He notes that: "rage" could mean "lust," and "thing" could mean "penis," so that if we dig down to the undermeaning, lines 3 and 4 suggest a sexual organ so aroused that it impedes action.

This hidden sexual content of the sonnet is the product of Booth's ingenuity. His gloss on "perfect ceremony" is unconvincing. "Great prerogative" is not the same as "perfect ceremony." One does not "say" sexual intercourse. A better sense for "perfect ceremony" can be found.

A wholly different context has been discovered in Sonnet 23 by Germaine Greer. In a spirited effort to give due recognition to Anne Shakespeare, Greer has suggested that the addressee of Sonnet 23 is Shakespeare's wife. *Greer* 259-260. The suggestion boldly breaks from the conventional assumption as to the addressee. It offers a new scenario in which the poet repents his sexual infidelities and seeks his spouse's forgiveness. It supposes that "the perfect ceremony" is the marital union. Plausible as this account is, it stretches too far in giving this meaning to "perfect ceremony." A spouse does not "say" a marriage. An ongoing marriage is not a "perfect ceremony." Nor can the original exchange of vows be meant. A wedded man could not forget to say what he's already said.

The Plea. We cannot name the someone to whom the sonnet is addressed; that it is someone is a necessary inference from its plea to its addressee to listen. It is not a solitary colloquy addressed to the

poet himself. Not every reader will respond or is expected to. The
poem speaks to the same person or persons to whom Shakespeare has
addressed the *Loves Martyr* poem. The addressee is a co-believer.

Sonnet 23 has at its core

So I for fear of trust forget to say

The perfect ceremony of love's rite.

In what sense can one forget out of fear? It would seem that
"forget" is defensive. The poet is admitting that he has failed in his
duty, something that might happen out of the conflict of fear and rage
expressed in the opening four lines. The speaker has failed in what
duty? To say a ceremony. Although to a modern ear a priest says
mass while a layman prays at it, the use of "say" to mean any recitation
of a prescribed form was standard sixteenth century English. *O.E.D.*
vol. 14, 546-547 at "say" 9a; so, today, one says his prayers. What does
the speaker fail to say? It's part of a ritual; so it is probably ecclesiastical.
It's "the perfect ceremony" of the ritual of love. In the canon of the
mass, at its most solemn moment, the celebrant proclaims the oblation
he offers to be "perfect." The mass is a rite of love. The deficiency of
the speaker, fearful and angry, has been his failure to pray the mass – to
express his own love and to respond to the great love extended to him.

Two autobiographical analogies are advanced to illuminate the
poet's position. In the first, he is like a young actor struck by stage
fright. In the second, Greene's image of a wounded tiger may come to
mind. The author of *Titus Andronicus* has known outrage and the anger
caused by outrage to the point that his strength has paradoxically been
weakened. The analogies are personal and defensive. They lessen the
poet's guilt as to what he forgot to say.

On line 5, "for fear of trust," *Booth* 151 notes Shakespeare's interest
in the complex compound of fear and trust and offers three alternative
meanings:

"(1) afraid to trust myself; (2) afraid of responsibility; (3) afraid that I will not be trusted." Each alternative plausibly applies if the poet is addressing a particular beloved. With equal or greater plausibility if the poet is speaking to a co-believer, he admits that (1) he (a backslider) fears he won't be trusted; (2) he fears taking responsibility; (3) he fears to trust himself; and (4) he fears being trusted (and so brought into dangerous company).

The poet concludes with the request that his writings be read as speaking for him and that they be read with the insights that love will provide. If "love" sometimes refers to the God who is love, while sometimes it designates a human emotion, love in Sonnet 23 is ambiguous or, in other words, a pun. It refers to what love of a human being may discover in the sonnets. It also refers to the love expressed in the mass. The appeal to hear with love's eyes suggests that there is more to be found than what first meets the eye.

The love of God, who Himself is love, was at the heart of Counter-Reformation piety. The place of love in the theology of the Jesuit missionaries to England is captured in these lines of Robert Southwell:

> I praise him most, I love him best, all praise and love is his.
> With him I love, in him I love, and cannot live amisse.

Loves sweetest mark, lawdes highest theme, mans most desired light:

> To love him, life; to leave him, death; to live in him, delighte.
>   "A childe my Choyce," *St. Robert*, p.12.

Why is the love in Sonnet 23 characterized as "silent"? Surely the sonnets speak continually of love. The characterization is Shakespearean exaggeration. The love that is silent has, like Lavinia in *Titus Adronicus*, had its tongue forcibly removed. It cannot be openly expressed. The aptness and urgency of the sonnet's plea will be apparent to anyone open to reading the Twenty-two in the context of Shakespeare's community and his own celebration of Love's martyr. Construed this way, Sonnet 23 is an invitation to the spiritual reading of all Twenty-two. It is the trusted co-believer who is conjured to hear with the eye.

Nonetheless, I do not adopt this interpretation. My reason: the addressee is too indefinite, the invitation too broad, the context uncertain. Let us stay with sonnets whose addressees are identifiable and limited.

Guides. Sequence, proximity, and linkage are guides. Their early dating not only isolates the first seventeen from the next one hundred and thirty-seven but emphasizes how long Shakespeare had practiced sonnet-writing before the sonnets were published in 1609.

The closing line of Sonnet 94 also occurs in the speech of the king in *Edward III*:

Lilies that fester smell far worse than weeds.

King Edward III 2.1.516.

As 1595 is the known date for the play, it can be guessed that the sonnet was written then or earlier; but it is no more than a guess. In 1598, Francis Meres referred to Shakespeare's "sugared sonnets among his private friends." *Edmondson and Wells* 3. In 1599, versions of Sonnets 138 and 141 were published in the second edition of *The Passionate Pilgrim*. See *Cohen* 1923; hence, nineteen or more were substantially done a decade before all one hundred and fifty-four emerged.

After the first seventeen, the addressees of the sonnets are speculative. Proximity appears to be the critics' principal interpretive tool. For example, *Greenblatt* 237-239 treats Sonnet 18, "Shall I compare thee to a summer's day" as addressed to Southampton or whichever youth is the addressee of Sonnets 1-17: Shakespeare, the messenger in the first seventeen sonnets, has now fallen in love with the teenager he was supposed to persuade to marry. That deduction assumes that the order of the poems' placement is decisive.

That the order is not decisive is indicated in two ways. First, some of the sonnets are incomplete. Sonnet 146, "Poor soul, the center of my sinful earth," lacks part of its second line; the printer has had to fill it in by duplicating the last four words of the first line. Sonnet 126, "O thou, my lovely boy, who in thy pow'r," is without lines 13 and 14, the couplet necessary to complete a sonnet. The printer has emphasized the missing lines by putting pairs of parentheses surrounding blanks where the lines should be. These gaps are evidence that the printing went ahead of what Shakespeare himself approved. Second, there is the curious placing of Sonnet 145, "Those lips that love's own hand did make." The woman so saluted says, "I hate." But seeing the poet's distress,

I hate from hate away she threw,

And saved my life saying, not you.

"Hate away," it is argued, is a pun on Hathaway; the poem celebrates Shakespeare's first love and only wife, Anne Hathaway. It's hard to deny the pun. *Booth* 500 notes that it has been pointed out and adds that "And" in the last line might have been pronounced "Anne," so that it, too, plays on the name of Shakespeare's wife. He further remarks that Sonnet 145 is the only one in tetrameter. He considers the possibility that it may not even be by Shakespeare but appears to accept its authenticity. Sonnet 145 remains for him "the slightest of the sonnets." Once the pun or puns are taken into account it is difficult to see a chronological order followed in the sonnet sequence. Wells, taking the same position on the addressee of Sonnet 145, adds that Sonnet 27 "Weary with toil I haste me to my bed" "could even" be addressed to Anne. *Wells, 2010* 64.

Other sonnets are addressed to a woman the speaker knows when he is no longer an "untutored youth": e.g., Sonnet 138, "When my love swears that she is made of truth." This woman, whose "false-speaking tongue" is here remarked, may be found in a number of the poems if one pictures the sonnets as the story of a love affair. Other sonnets are as unmistakably addressed to a man, e.g., Sonnet 20, "A woman's face, with nature's own hand painted." The next line suggests a homosexual attraction

Hast thou, the master mistress of my passion . . .

The poem goes on to cancel this suggestion:

And for a woman wast thou first created,

Till nature as she wrought thee fell a-doting

And by addition me of thee defeated,

By adding one thing to my purpose nothing.

For those who simplify the sonnets, the poems divide into "two main sections," the first one hundred and twenty-six on the youth supposed to reappear again and again as the object of erotic desire, and the last twenty-eight on the mistress. But as Walter Cohen remarks, this "standard simplification," is adopted although "the vast majority of the poems" do not designate the sex of the person discussed. *Cohen* 1919. The bulk of the poems associated with any love affair are only by inference connected with the poems in which gender is declared. Inferences of this kind are not implausible but not infallible.

The conventional division assumes that every sonnet after Sonnet 126 must be related to a woman. But why, if Shakespeare could address erotic poetry to a man? A large number of sonnets in the second part do not identify gender by either a pronoun or a noun. Sonnets 130, 132, 133, 134, 135, 136, 137, 140, 142, 147, 148, and 150 could relate to a woman or a man; the argument for saying that they relate to a woman depends on proximity to sonnets with an unmistakable feminine reference and often incorporates the assumption that the sonnets are telling a story about one unlucky affair with one woman – an assumption not shown to be accurate. In the first section of the standard division, Sonnet 78 could relate either to a man or a woman. Sonnet 1-17 can be put aside as a block known to have a male addressee. If the strict criteria of requiring a pronoun or a specific gendered norm like "boy" or "mistress" are adopted, the remaining sonnets that identify gender are as follows: To a male addressee: 20, 41, 42 and 54. About a male subject: Sonnets 33, 39, 44, 63, 67, 68, 108. Add the first seventeen and there is a total of 28 sonnets bearing on a man. A female addressee is explicitly in view in Sonnets 138, 139, and 141; a woman is the subject of Sonnets 127 (arguably), 128, 130, 145, 151, 153, and 154 – a total of ten bearing on a woman. If we arbitrarily assign the ambiguous Sonnets 53 and 78 to a man and the equally unspecific Sonnets 130-137, 140, 142, 147, 148, and 150 to a woman, the number of gender-related rises to twenty two related to a female and thirty related to a man. But seventeen of those addressed to a man are not expressions of the poet's own love for the addressee. Subtract them, and thirteen sonnets relate to a man.

The numbers could be swelled by adding to them "linked sonnets," that is, those which immediately precede or follow sonnets where gender is apparent and whose content is closely related to the gender-apparent sonnet. Linkages are indisputable. They suffer as a guide to the poetry from Shakespeare's quickness to associate ideas. The linkage of one poem to another may turn not on an identity of subject but on a similarity of situation. In particular instances, the connection must be a matter of judgment. More connections are likely to be discerned by those who assume that the conventional simplification is correct; their assumption is confirmed for them by their discernment of a linkage.

Linked sonnets exist in clusters. The clusters are not continuous. One cannot get from Sonnet 18 to Sonnet 126 or from Sonnet 127 to

Sonnet 154 by a series of interconnections. As far as the argument of this book is concerned, the last point is capital. Space exists between the clusters. Only the simplification of the Sonnets to two gendered subjects can obscure the vigorous variety of the poems. Arguments, no doubt, could be advanced for adding one or more to each category. Such additions would not change the fundamental fact that the great majority of the sonnets have no explicit connection with a man or a woman.

Language of lust, language of liturgy. The crux in fixing the addressees of the Twenty-two is the expression of total devotion. All of the Sonnets are, in the felicitous phrase of line 209 of *A Lover's Complaint*, "deep-brained," that is, thought-out with extraordinary care; complex creations. Whether or not this poem's author is Shakespeare – its authenticity is accepted by Kerrigan and vigorously denied by Vickers – the poem assumes that a sonnet may accompany and enrich a gift from a lover to the beloved. As the same poem – annexed to the Sonnets in the quarto of 1609 – demonstrates, the symbols and vocabulary of the sacred may be used to express profane love: "oblation," for example, is made to signify the gifts that a seducer is offering the target of the seduction:

> That is, to you my origin and ender,
>
> For these of force must your oblation be
>
> Since I their altar, you empatron me
>
> *A Lover's Complaint* 222-225.

Crammed into these three lines is the deification of the beloved, who is addressed as if she were God, the Alpha and the Omega; or as if she were the patron saint of the man, who declares that he is her altar; or as if she were the offeree of a total sacrifice made by the man himself, who presents his gifts as an oblation. The extravagance of the language suggests satire or that the author is piling up the images that a seasoned and hypocritical scoundrel would employ; and such a scoundrel is, in fact, the object of the lover's complaint. That sacred imagery may serve sinister ends scarcely proves that the poet of the Sonnets when expressing his own deep emotions perverts the ordinary sacred sense.

The choice of interpretations is sometimes between taking the words of a sonnet in a normal sense or construing them as the idolatrous, unrestrained language of a person beside himself with passion. Undoubtedly, one gripped by love or under the sway of uncontrollable lust may engage in all sorts of bizarre behavior and imagine more. From the multitude of instances, I take one example from the life of an author, a second from the life of a modern woman, and a third from the life of a judge. In his sixties, Samuel Johnson addressed a letter to Mrs. Thrale (a letter in French because of his embarrassment) asking that "vous me tiennez dans l'esclavage que savez si bien rendre heureaux." *Bate* 439-440. The letter which could be described as childlike or as masochistic is a large departure from Johnson's self-image as a masculine man of robust common sense; his use of French may be read as a way of giving himself room to abase himself. The second example: a spirited graduate of Oxford, Jennifer Williams, in the 1930's wrote to Herbert Hart, the future jurisprudent and her eventual husband: "Lord of my love . . . I will become landlord, tenant, slave, cook, whore, anything you like." *Lacey* 68. Not a lifetime commitment but an apt expression of a masochistic moment. As for the judge, it is a modern instance. Chief Judge of the Court of Appeals of New York, he became obsessed with a young relative who spurned him; he committed the federal crime of threatening to kidnap her daughter. He was removed from the highest judicial office in the state to a cell in a federal penitentiary. See the *New York Times*, September 10, 1993. But why multiply examples? Every observant and self-observant person knows that passion may produce extreme statements and extraordinary emotions and deeds. Shakespeare's sonnets do not exceed the ordinary extraordinary. The reader must still discriminate between the loves that they make manifest. That Shakespeare was reduced to idolatry or to infantile posturing is not inconceivable. Still, the burden must be on those who seek to prove such disorientation expressed in language entirely open to a rational, if religious, meaning.

Shakespeare can deliberately deploy sacred images to express true secular love, as Romeo does in wooing Juliet:

> O then, dear saint, let lips do what hands do,
>
> They pray, grant thou, lest faith turn to despair.
>
> *Romeo and Juliet* 1.5.100-101.

To Romeo, the playwright provides the passionate words of an impetuous youth. Is a sonnet like 125 "Were't ought to me that I bore the canopy" different if he is speaking for himself? The language is not decisive. The poet who does not shrink from hyperbolic manipulation of the language of religious devotion in the case of his creations may not shrink from doing the same in his own behalf. But what is decisive in Sonnet 125 is the concluding couplet banishing the informer. This sinister figure figures as a danger not to romantic love but to prohibited piety.

My approach in part coincides with that of Stanley Wells and Paul Edmondson, who in their edition of the Sonnets came to the conclusion that "critical thought about the poems has been bedeviled by a number of misconceptions." Wells proceeds to set out "the three principal ones" – first, that Shakespeare determined the sequence; second, that sonnets 1-126 are all addressed to a male; and (3) that each reference to a man is to the same man. As Wells sees, the Sonnets are a miscellany not a narrative. *Wells, 2010* 64-65. Where I disagree with past "critical thought" and with Wells and Edmondson is in finding addressees other than lovers or close friends.

Caveats. Some sonnets that I have failed to discover may be patient of a spiritual reading. I don't pretend to have exhausted the possibilities with the Twenty-two. If such sonnets are identified, they will, I believe, only confirm the spiritual readings advanced of the Twenty-two.

The Twenty-two are not set apart or labeled in the sonnet sequence. Readers may well find my arguments persuasive as to some, unconvincing as to others; given the subjective judgments involved, the number may shrink or expand. Hence, I don't press the argument that twenty-two is one-seventh of the sequence as if the Lord was honored one day out of seven. I note the possibility and do not rely on it.

The chapter headings that follow are obviously of my choosing, deployed to identify, more blatantly than the poet did, the addressees of the poems. Ascertainment of the addressees does not determine the meaning of the Twenty-two, only their direction. Taken all together, the one hundred and fifty-four show Shakespeare as an anguished, doubting, hopeful, remorseful, sinful, triumphant, loving creature. The sonnets convey all that complexity. That is not their purpose. Each is a communication from the poet to a particular audience. To accomplish the communication, the sonnets have a structure. Within the structure, a climax occurs, a point is emphasized. The sonnets are not soundbites, reducible to that single point. Nonetheless, to concentrate on the complex of emotions, to skirt the structure, and to downplay the climactic point is to misread the sonnet. In the case of the Twenty-two the structure contains a spiritual context within which the poet breathes, within which the concluding couplet confirms his commitment to love.

I do not pretend to reduce the Twenty-two to a single meaning. They are full of the tensions that have made them so open to interpretation. But I do maintain that without putting them into the context of Shakespeare's upbringing, community and poetry in honor of the Lines, and without ascertaining the particular addressees, the full range of Shakespeare's meaning is lost. Rightly read, these sonnets are recovered from the dead hand of conventional criticism and become alive. In the most personal of these sonnets, I believe, Shakespeare, in his own words, offers himself to God "an oblation poor but free."

6. Two to His Soul

I begin with two poems resistant to any romantic reading:

Sonnet 129.
"Th' expense of spirit in a waste of shame"

Th' expense of Spirit in a waste of shame
Is lust in action, and till action, lust
Is perjur'd, murderous, bloody, full of blame,
Savage, extreme, rude, cruel, not to trust,
Enjoy'd no sooner but despised straight,
Past reason hunted, and no sooner had,
Past reason hated, as a swallow'd bait,
On purpose laid to make the taker mad:
Mad in pursuit and in possession so,
Had, having, and in quest to have extreme,
A bliss in proof, and prov'd, a very woe,
Before, a joy propos'd; behind, a dream.
All this the world well knows, yet none knows well
To shun the heaven that leads men to this hell.

Sonnet 146.
"Poor soul, the centre of my sinful earth"

Poor soul, the centre of my sinful earth,
My sinful earth these rebel powers array,
Why dost thou pine within and suffer dearth,
Painting thy outward walls so costly gay?
Why so large cost, having so short a lease,
Dost thou upon thy fading mansion spend?
Shall worms, inheritors of this excess,
Eat up thy charge? Is this thy body's end?
Then soul, live thou upon thy servant's loss,
And let that pine to aggravate thy store;
Buy terms divine in selling hours of dross;
Within be fed, without be rich no more:
So shall thou feed on death, that feeds on men,
And death once dead, there's no more dying then.

Dialogue was an established way of instruction in classical antiquity and adapted by Christian writers. Isidore of Seville, for example, in his sixth century *Synonyma de lamentatione aninae peceatoris, Patrologia latina* 83, 825 presented a sinner arguing with his reason. Dialogues between soul and body were numerous in medieval Europe. *Bertarnd*, col. 841.

Unlike the other spiritual sonnets, Sonnet 146 begins with the addressee stated in the first line: the poet's soul. In apparent

contradiction of my general argument, Sonnet 129 has no visible
addressee and at most an indirect and intangible one. I argue that 146
and 129 cohere and should be read together, beginning with 146. It is
cast in an established medieval mode as a dialogue between the soul
and the body. *Booth* 501. "Poor soul" refers to "the immortal spirit
of the speaker." *Id.* 502. It is always dangerous in the law to say that
a proposition is undisputed and even more dangerous to assert that it
is indisputable. The same cautions hold for literary criticism. A new
angle can always be found. Let me only say, then, that I don't know of
any serious challenge to Booth's reading of "Poor soul."

In the portion of *Edward III* almost certainly written by
Shakespeare, the union of, and distinction between, soul and body is
expressed by the countess of Salisbury as she repulses the "lascivious"
king's advances:

> As easy may my intellectual soul
>
> be lent away and yet my body lives,
>
> as lend my body, palace to my soul
>
> away from her and yet retain my soul.
>
> *Edward III* 2.1.590-594.

The body is a habitat, here a very fine one, it cannot be put to sinful
use without endangering its inhabitant.

To many neurologists today the soul would be poor because it
has disappeared from scientific discourse. For Shakespeare, as for
Christians before and since, the soul was a substantial reality. With
this meaning in the poet's mind, Sonnet 146 is a straightforward
exhortation to Shakespeare's spirit to lead the life of a Christian. The
climax in Lines 13-14 incorporates the central, sustaining Christian
belief; death is not the end:

So when this corruptible hath put on incorruption, and this hath
put on immortaltie, then shal be brought to passage the saying that

is wryten, Death is swalowed up unto victorie. Death, where is thy stinge, grave where is thy victorie? 1 Cor 15: 54-55.

St. Paul's challenge to the finality of death has resounded since about 58 A.D. It espousers a belief and a triumphant hope.

A range of responses to the poem is noted by Booth. For many readers, it is "a statement of Shakespeare's sympathetic attitude towards a commonplace of Christian doctrine." *Booth* 511, quoting R.C. Southham. For the poet John Crowe Ransom, "the divine terms which the soul buys are "not particularly Christian;" they are Platonic. *Id.*, 511. Ransom also suggested that lines 7, 8 and 11, if taken literally, were cannibalistic. Booth himself at 514 argues for preserving the complexity of the poem by seeing different and opposing elements within it, unsimplified to any single Christian theme.

These diverse views do not take us far. Southam's report of readers finding "sympathy" for "Christian commonplaces" is deadening – the ho-hum of a man who has heard it all at Sunday school and retained little more than adages. Ransom's comments, made orally, do not diminish the Christian content. No one, except in literary badinage, could suppose the metaphor of feeding was literal. Platonism was in the air first century Christians' breathed. As for the divine terms offered the soul, the Gospel of Matthew reports:

"Again, the kyngdom of heaven is like to a merchant ý seeketh good pearles, Which when he had found one of great price, went and sold all that he had, and boght it." Matthew 13:45-46.

The deal for the pearl is not recommended by Christ?

Reporting but not endorsing the critics quoted, Booth himself seeks to find complications in the imagery of the sonnet. The servant of line 9, he suggests, permits the reader to think of "real business relationships" in which the master exploits the servant. Similarly, the short-term tenant of lines 3-5, he says, may bring to mind the exploitation of renters in real life. *Id.* 515. Neither example is convincing. The Elizabethan world, reflected in Shakespeare's plays, did not have a Marxist sense of servants as an exploited class. As for the short-term tenant, he is indulgently decorating the property. Who's complaining?

In the end, Booth concludes, the relation of body and soul in the poem accords with "our impression of Christian doctrine." *Id.* 516. Impression? It is pure Paul. Not all Christian doctrine is contained in these fourteen lines. There is no reference to redemption, resurrection, or Christ. Any Christian would supply the references and know why death has no sting. The rhetorical challenge of death is a Christian manifesto, no less in the sonnet than in Paul.

Rufus Wainwright's take on Sonnet 129, *supra*, chapter 4, is very different from that of a seasoned scholar of the poet's work, who writes in 2010, that this sonnet "expresses the bitter self-contempt of one who castigates himself for having yielded to lust." *Wells*, p 116.

Line 1 of Sonnet 129, "Th' expense of spirit in a waste of shame" strikes the theme that pervades the poem. Shakespeare focuses on the paradox – spirit is expended in unlawful sexual action. A comparable use of "expense" occurs in Sonnet 94, *infra.*, where the celibates refrain from such expenditure. A standard Christian note is struck in the condemnation of sexual lust as

Mad in pursuit, and in possession so

Booth spends several pages on phrases and individual words in the poem without attempting to relate it to any putative object of the poet's desire and without nominating anyone as addressee. It could be said that the poem was just Shakespeare expressing self-disgust at a life he once had led. Its placement only three sonnets after the start of the poems to the lady supposed to be the subject in the second part of the sonnets is awkward for the conventional critics. Why this heartfelt blast at mad passion so early in the affair?

I see the poem not as self-expression or helpless acknowledgment that passion must prevail. It is a speech to the poet's soul: Don't be a fool, don't pursue a deceptive dream, even though the wit and will to escape the trap are lacking. What is not mentioned as missing is the grace of God, the divine terms spoken of in 146, pointing to a way out of the hell held to be inescapable in 129.

Could these two poems be commissioned verse? I don't see how the possibility can be excluded that Shakespeare sought to express another person's spiritual distress or hope. Intensity of the emotions is not a certificate of sincerity. But whether written for another, or, as I prefer to believe, for himself, the two poems to the soul express Christian remorse and reconciling hope.

The most obvious point about these two poems, and the point most readily overlooked or brushed aside by conventional critics, is that neither is a love poem. On that account, they do not fit the conventional presentations of the sonnets. They are surds in the standard story. Their unexplained existence confirms the need for reconsideration of the remaining 152. May there not be more than two spiritual sonnets?

7. Three to Jesuits On Mission

Three poems have addressees identifiable among Shakespeare's known contemporaries:

Sonnet 69.
"Those parts of thee that the world's eye doth view"

Those parts of thee that the world's eye doth view
Want nothing that the thought of hearts can mend;
All tongues--the voice of souls--give thee that due,
Uttering bare truth, even so as foes Commend.
Their outward thus with outward praise is crown'd;
But those same tongues, that give thee so thine own,
In other accents do this praise confound
By seeing farther than the eye hath shown.
They look into the beauty of thy mind,
And that in guess they measure by thy deeds;
Then—churls—their thoughts (although their eyes
were kind)

To thy fair flower add the rank smell of weeds:
But why thy odour matcheth not thy show,
The soil is this, that thou dost common grow.

Sonnet 70.
"That thou art blam'd shall not be thy defect"

That thou art blam'd shall not be thy defect,
For slander's mark was ever yet the fair;
The ornament of beauty is suspect,
A Crow that flies in heaven's sweetest air.
So thou be good, slander doth but approve
Their worth the greater being woo'd of time;
For Canker vice the sweetest buds doth love,
And thou present'st a pure unstained prime.
Thou hast passed by the ambush of young days
Either not assail'd, or victor being charg'd;
Yet this thy praise cannot be so thy praise,
To tie up envy, evermore enlarg'd,
If some suspect of ill mask'd not thy show,
Then thou alone kingdoms of hearts shouldst owe.

Sonnet 94.
"They that have power to hurt, and will do none"

They that have power to hurt, and will do none,
That do not do the thing they most do show,
Who, moving others, are themselves as stone,
Unmoved, cold, and to temptation slow;
They rightly do inherit heaven's graces,
And husband nature's riches from expense;
They are the lords and owners of their faces,
Others, but stewards of their excellence.
The summer's flow'r is to the summer sweet,
Though to itself it only live and die,
But if that flower with base infection meet,
The basest weed outbraves his dignity:
For sweetest things turn sourest by their deeds,
Lilies that fester, smell far worse than weeds.

The human beings to whom these three sonnets are addressed are entirely distinct from the young male commonly taken as the target. The supposition that Shakespeare is tucking a single individual into a class so that he can make generalizations is a weak evasion of the entire thrust of the three poems. They speak of the reaction of people to a group, and they speak to a group. The theme of the third of these is clearest.

This sonnet, 94 "They that have power to hurt, and will do none," has as its subject those who have an unexercised power and yet move others; who are moved by the austerity of their manners. They wear a dress that does not jibe with their acts. They are heirs of the grace of God. Yet they are the subject of slander. They require a sharp warning delivered as a climax in the concluding couplet. As the poem is more closely examined, these unidentified figures take on the shape and situation of the Jesuits in England.

The memoir of John Gerard reflects the situation. In many households, the Jesuits are welcome; they give the *Spiritual Exercises* of St. Ignatius; they bring back people to the Church or make converts. Yet some of the old priests, that is, those ordained in England before the accession of Elizabeth, regard them "as meddlesome innovators." Later, in the 1590's, hostility to them has been aroused by "the quarrels that have broken out between us and a section of the secular clergy." The government is "anxious to crush the more uncompromising party." *Gerard* 28.

Counseling Catholic gentry and nobility, keeping contact with the continent, the Jesuits were well-placed to do harm. The government thought they did it. The poet acknowledges the suspicion and denies that it is founded. What "they most do show" is their outer garment, the soutane, from which the popular sobriquet for them, "crows," is derived. Crows, as already noted in chapter 3, are classed with kites as birds of prey by Shakespeare in *Coriolanus* 4.5.41-43. The crows of the sonnet do not act as birds of prey. The paradox in the reference to their dress – "the thing they most do show" – is inexplicable if the reputation of crows is disregarded.

They are self-controlled "owners of their faces," while others acting only as stewards dispense what they have brought. They direct the others; they are "themselves as stone." People are drawn to them "as metal to the magnet." *Booth* 306, quoting Philip Martin. They are more than austere. They are celibate. As Shakespeare, enjoying the paradox puts it, they "husband nature's riches from expense." Husbands in their celibacy, they do not squander seed in intercourse. "Expense" is used as in Sonnet 129 where fornication is an "expense of spirit in a waste of shame." *Booth* 307 catches a sexual implication in "nature's riches." However, he makes no attempt to elucidate the sense of line 6. Resourceful as he is, he has found no way to explain in his terms this celebration of the celibate. Not to notice this key characteristic of the men is to overlook a key to the poem.

These disciplined ascetics recall the meek who in Matthew's Gospel 5.5 "inherit the earth." Varying the phrase, the poet praises them as rightly inheriting the graces given by God. The summer's flower will live and die without reproducing. It lives only "to itself." Yet it is sweet in the season of its life. "The summer's flow'r" is rhymed with "pow'r", connecting the two. The first phrase is a literal translation of *flos aetatis*, employed in Catullus to mean virginity. *Id.* 307. Self-contained, these men are "cold and to temptation slow." They observe their vow of chastity. The poet echoes the exhortation of St. Paul "to live and die" to the Lord. Romans 14:7-8. *Booth* 305-306 reacts negatively to the singular qualities attributed to these monk-like persons. To him the qualitites are "repellant." That is not how Shakespeare views them. The men so characterized are unstintingly praised: they "rightly do inherit heaven's graces."

After the praise comes the warning in the somber last two lines. If their flower "with base infection meet" – that is, if their virginity is corrupted or, more broadly, if they use their power to do harm – the result will be disastrous. They could do what would be self-destructive. "The corruption of the best is the worst," as the proverb has it. Their reputation would have a stench.

Most readers will register surprise that the group described in Sonnet 94 is also the addressee. Sonnets are seen as one-on-one. But the warning of the last four lines is empty if it is not implicitly addressed to those who are admired and yet may fail.

A recent chronicler of "the Shakespeare wars" has noted that, then a doctoral student at Harvard, Booth chose this sonnet to pulverize the exegesis of William Empson, who had treated its subject as a single young man, the beloved of the poet. See *Rosenbaum* 468. Rosenbaum himself on meeting Booth thought he in person was like the single subject of the poem, a cool, serenely aloof figure. *Id*. Strikingly, Empson, Booth and Rosenbaum all construed the plurals of the poem as meant to cover one man.

The Arden editors detect in the opening line an echo of Sir John Salisbury's motto, *posse et nolle, nobile est* ("To be able and to refuse is noble"). *Duncan-Jones* 100. But the several persons indirectly spoken to by the sonnet cannot be reduced to one individual. They cannot be identified with those holding power in the government, for the latter are the actual rulers; nor with the clergy of the Church of England, who were married; nor with nuns, who did not exist in England. Clad, in the houses of their Catholic hosts, in their sable soutanes, moving their hosts' consciences by their direction, unmarried and preserving their vow, the addressees must be the missionaries who have come from abroad to maintain the faith.

Booth 307 observes apropos of line 10 that Romans 14:7-8 "is curiously relevant to this sonnet": The passage from St. Paul reads:

For none of us lyve to hym selfe; neither dothe any of us dye to him selfe.

For whether we lyve, we lyve unto the Lord; or whether we dye, we dye unto the Lord; whether we lyve therefore, or dye, we are the Lordes

Romans 14:7-8.

Booth proceeds to a short commentary on the biblical verses. He makes no attempt to integrate them into his understanding of the poem.

Sonnet 94 has the distinction of being "the most frequently interpreted of the sonnets." *Booth* 305. The reason, I suggest, is evident. As long as the addressees are not acknowledged, so long must the poem perplex.

Sonnets 69 and 70 belong together and relate to Sonnet 94. Sonnet 69 "Those parts of thee that the world's eye doth see" uses the second singular pronoun. The presumption is that a single person is the addressee. The presumption seems precarious. Why is one person the object of attention by a multitude of friends and foes?

The puzzle is solved if the "you" of the poem is not a person but a group. It is a group whose performance has won admiration. They look good. Heart's desire could not make them any better: lines 1 and 2. "All tongues" praise them, expressing their deepest feelings ("the voice of souls") and speaking the "bare truth." Even their enemies agree in the encomium. Yet there is tension. Those that praise the group ("the same tongues") harbor thoughts that are unkind ("churls") as they look more closely and "measure by thy deeds". The group has acquired an odor ("the rank smell of weeds"). The basis of this phenomenon is that the group has become too familiar, "hackneyed in the eyes of men," to borrow a phrase from Part I of *Henry IV*, 3.2.40. In John Gerard's words as he accounts for the hostility the Jesuits encounter, "The reason, I presume is, that our numbers have grown so much." *Gerard* 28.

The "you" addressed must, according to the conventional criticism, be the beloved young man. But how he wins the praise of all including his enemies, why the thoughts that suspect him are churlish, how he has become too familiar a phenomenon – these reactions of people to him are close to inexplicable. In contrast, these reactions are those of lay Catholics and government officials, who admired the brilliance of Campion and Southwell; now that the Jesuits in England have increased, the government thinks their actions are subversive and lay Catholics are uneasy.

Successful spiritual enterprises are capable of causing envy. The ardor of their adherents amazes the outsider and makes him suspect a sinister secret. In recent times, Opus Dei appears to have aroused such sentiments. The Abbey of Regina Laudis in Bethlehem Connecticut, a community of contemplative nuns, was the victim of a cloud of baseless rumors in the 1980's. What was emblematic of the Jesuits' virtue, their "fair flow'r," has added to it an ugly reputation. These suspicions are not accepted by the poet: these thoughts are churls. Why they have occurred is given an innocuous explanation, as in the saying "Familiarity breeds contempt."

In Line 14, "soil" is a pun, meaning "the ground" or "the blemish." Shakespeare used the same line in *Edward III*, 2.2.808. As already noted in chapter 4, it cannot be determined which came first, but if one sees Shakespeare drawing on something he has recently written, the coincidence of lines shows the sonnet to have been written in the 1590's in the period in which the play was written. More significant is the function of the line in the play. The words form part of Warwick's speech congratulating his daughter on not caving to the adulterous courtship of the king. The context can be captured in these lines that follow from the anxious father:

> and every glory that inclines to sin,
>
> the shame is treble by the opposite.

Id. 2.1.809-810.

That is to say, the sin in wrongly reaching for apparent glory, the king's patronage, would be the opposite of glorious, indeed triply shameful. The moral message delivered to the Jesuits in Line 14 is an analogous anxious exhortation to withstand temptation.

Sonnet 70 "That thou are blamed shall not be thy defect" repudiates the suspicions of Sonnet 69 as unjust, as the opening line declares and the second line drives home: "For slander's mark was ever yet the fair." The third line repeats this truth, and the fourth applies it specifically to a crow – an odd bird to illustrate the point until one recalls that in the *Loves Martyr* poem this bird stands defiantly for a Jesuit. But *Booth* 255 declines to read "an ornament of beauty" in apposition to "Crow" (capitalized in Q). He observes that beauty as a crow does not seem "reasonable." He reads "suspect" to mean "suspicion", and this noun is then read by him as apposite to "Crow." Grammatically, his argument works. It misses entirely the poem's praise of the Jesuits coupled to a note of warning about the risk their reputation runs. The force of line four is that the Jesuit acts "in heaven's sweetest air" but is seen by slanderous eyes as a crow in a negative literal sense. "the ornament of beauty" may be read as a reference to the special shine of the Jesuits: they embellish beauty; and beauty, as in the *Loves Martyr* poem, may stand for the Church.

Shakespeare does not stop with rebuking the slanderers. He turns to the Jesuits to warn them. Their group has begun well ("passed by the ambush of young days"). Now it is in its prime, "pure, unstained." The beginning to which the poem refers was, I should judge, the arrival of Campion and Persons. The prime is the present. As long as they are good, slander only sets off their true worth. Yet there is danger for them. The sweetest flowers attract cankers. The group cannot rest on the praise that they have received. Envy of them is "evermore enlarged." Suspicion of them remains. Line 14 is upbeat: "owe" means "own." *Booth* 257. If suspicion did not cloud their reputation, they would own the only kind of kingdom they should seek: that of hearts.

The thought of Sonnet 69, reinforced in Sonnet 70, and emphatically restated in Sonnet 94, is that the Jesuits in England are remarkable men, dedicated and disciplined; at the same time they have engendered envy, slander, and belief that they are up to no good. They must not be seen as seeking to win an earthly kingdom. What they can win by way of kingdoms are those of souls.

The printer of Q has been accused of sloppiness. He begins line 6 of Sonnet 69 with "Their" and line 5 of Sonnet 70 with "Their". Modern editors correct "their" to "thy." The correction appears to be necessary in Sonnet 70 and arguably better in Sonnet 69. But a printer twice confusing "Thy" with "Their" seems to me less likely than the poet himself using the plural as he thought of the group he had in mind.

The time that these three sonnets were composed must be pre-Gunpowder Plot. It is a time when the government is already speaking of Jesuit treason, but without the specifics of the Plot, nothing has happened to change Shakespeare's own high valuation of these men. Sharply and persistently he tells them of their peril if they do not stick to their spiritual agenda.

In the 1930's, two German artists associated with opponents of the Nazi regime produced prophetic paintings. Otto Dix in *Lot with His Daughters* (1939) "expressed the horrible presentiment of a burning Dresden, with the prominent silhouettes of the Frauenkirche and the Hofkirche." Even earlier in 1936, in the central panel of Hans Grundig's triptych *The Thousand-year Reich*, "images of a destroyed city appeared, anticipating the reality of 13 February 1945, more horrible than the most horrible vision." *The Splendor of Dresden* 62.

Like the German artists, Shakespeare sees as in a prophetic dream how the Jesuits will look if they are ever seen to seem to mix with treason. The details do not have the color of the artists' images. Enough is said to be a warning. The Gunpowder Plot, as it was exploited by the government, gave realization to Shakespeare's forebodings.

The events of 1605. The events of 1605 are of marginal relevance to Sonnets 69, 70 and 94 as confirming the power of the poet's prophetic soul. The events are of the highest relevance as reasons why the poet would not have wanted his association with the Jesuits publicly established. After 1605, the odor of the Jesuits in England was bad.

In chapter 2, I gave an account of the pilgrimage in August 1605 of the four Jesuits (Garnet, Gerard, Oldcorne, and Tesimond), Sir Everard Digby and Lady Rookwood and noted that Garnet stayed en route with John Grant and Robert Wintour. No judge could have found that the pilgrimage in itself was criminal. Any government probing associations that would suggest conspiracy would have found these connections suspicious and would have noted that the pilgrimage took place little more than three months before discovery of the Plot.

The Gunpowder Plot, in the government's view, demonstrated the Jesuits' criminality. To make its point, the government tortured the Jesuit superior, Henry Garnet. Garnet then revealed his prior knowledge of the Plot, acquired he said under the seal of confession and so not communicable. *Caraman* 381-383. His belated admissions with a half-apology unpersuasive with his interrogators was enough to hang him. And to hang him not only by the neck but in reputation.

Does Shakespeare accept Garnet's guilt? *Asquith* 220 has spiritedly argued that he does not. The argument turns on references in the knocking-on-the-door scene in *Macbeth, Act 2, scene 3.* The porter of hell first welcomes "a farmer who hangs himself in the expectation of plenty." "Farmer" was a Garnet alias. As the knocking continues, Shakespeare arguably doubled the allusion to Garnet, known for his defense of equivocation:

Faith, here's an equivocator could swear on both the scales against either scale, who committed treason enough for God's sake, yet could not equivocate to heaven, O come in, equivocator.

Macbeth 2.3.0-12.

The allusion to Garnet is unmistakable and does not seem friendly, unless one reads the treason having been for God's sake. The porter equivocates. Is there not a hint of self-reflection by the playwright? What is an equivocator but a punster? Who was the greatest punster of them all?

That Shakespeare was, at the least, ambivalent about Garnet is suggested by another passage. As Lady Macbeth steels herself to commit murder, she prays

> That my thick knife see not the wounds it makes
>
> Nor heaven peep through the blanket of the dark
>
> To cry 'Hold, hold.'

Macbeth 1.5.50-52.

It is plausibly suggested that "hold, hold" is an echo of the shout of a crowd sympathetic to Garnet as he struggled on the scaffold. *Jonathan Bate* 324.

The Sonnets were published three years after the government had put Garnet at the center of the conspiracy. But the Sonnets go no further than apprehension of what might happen. They do not pronounce judgment. They have not been updated to the time of publication. Something of what happened in 1605 was anticipated by our author, whose admiration for the subjects of the three sonnets is tempered only by the thought of what could go wrong.1

8. *The Church Speaks*

Sonnet 73.
"That time of year thou mayst in me behold"

That time of year thou mayst in me behold
When yellow leaves, or none, or few, do hang
Upon those boughs which shake against the cold,
Bare ruin'd choirs, where late the sweet birds sang.
In me thou see'st the twilight of such day
As after Sunset fadeth in the West,
Which by and by black night doth take away,
Death's second self, that seals up all in rest.
In me thou see'st the glowing of such fire,
That on the ashes of his youth doth lie,
As the death-bed, whereon it must expire,
Consum'd with that which it was nourish'd by.
  This thou perceiv'st, which makes thy love more strong,
  To love that well, which thou must leave ere long.

<u>Three Misinterpretations</u>:

(1) The speaker is speaking to a young man he loves, addressing him first with "an appeal of physical pathos (ruin) and then an appeal of mental decline (fading light)." *Vendler* 336.

(2) "the birds' recent song, now no longer heard, seems to refer to the speaker's own poetic voice." *Cohen* 1947.

(3) "a poem about old age." *Booth* 260.

Unless one imagines Shakespeare to have continued an affair with a younger man into a senescence that began before the poet was forty, no basis exists for applying the shaky boughs to a human being or for stretching a reference to ruined church architecture so that it stands for bodily decay. As a metaphor for an impaired body, a decayed church is an awkward, even a grotesque image. Still less is there reason to find after-sunset light to be a metaphor for Alzheimer's. It is equally unlikely that the Sonnets, which speak with sharp specificity, should include one that is merely a meditation on aging.

The crux for interpretation is identification of the speaker. It is my argument that the speaker is the Church herself. Precedent pointed to similar speakers in devotional works.

In the Hebrew prophets, God engaged in dialogue with his people, as, for example

> Now listen what I will do to my vineyard
>
> I will take away its fences and let it be barren
>
> > Isaiah 4:5
>
> I will state my case against my people
>
> for all the wrong they have done in forsaking me
>
> > Jeremiah 1:16

The piety of the Christian era assembled quotations of Jesus in the Gospels, presenting them as "the voice of Christ" and concluding:

> The words which I have spoken to you are spirit and life.
>
> > *The Imitation of Christ* 4, c.1

In Sonnet 73, the Body of Christ speaks.

<u>Interpretation</u>:

Lines 1-3. The weather is turning cold for the Church. After approximately one thousand years on English soil, frost foreshadowing winter has struck her. Her members are none or, on second thought, few. They are aged as autumn leaves are yellow.

Line 4. Choirs are "where services are sung." *Booth* 254. Where once the monks sang, there are ruins. The destruction of the monasteries is commemorated along with the music made by their former inhabitants. The battering the Church has received has laid her low.

The eminent historian, Eamon Duffy, has recently written: "Few human enterprises are more certainly doomed than the attempt to provide precise historical exposition of Shakespeare's Sonnets: those most elusive of poems defeat and will no doubt continue to defeat all attempts to decipher the story or stories they tell, or to identify the contemporary allusions they might be held to make, and Sonnet 73 is no exception." *Duffy 2003*, 40-41. This prophecy forms the introduction to an essay by Duffy on the cultural residue of Catholicism and the nostalgia evoked by the physical remains of England's past. Concentrating on the choirs, Duffy says Sonnet 73 could have been written by an Anglican highly sympathetic to the old religion. *Id.* 55-56. But the poet's presentation is of the Church consumed in the death of her martyrs. It is that perception, as line 13 declares, that makes the poet's love more strong. No Anglican would have had reason to speak in the voice of the dying Church.

Lines 5-8. "Death's second self" = sleep. *Booth* 254. It's time for the Church to sleep. The magnificent metaphor of line six where the Church is the sinking sun contains within it a hope, or rather a certainty: the sun also rises.

Lines 9-12. Life remains. A fire feeds this life at the same time that the fire consumes this life, as the martyrs give life to the Church as they die. Their love nourishes the Church while their deaths consume her. *Booth* 260 comments on "the contrariness that the poem manifests throughout." He offers no convincing reason for this contrariness. The contrary or, rather, paradoxical character of the poem comes from this: the Church lives in the deaths of the martyrs.

Line 13. The addressee, presumably the poet, sees this paradoxical phenomenon and, while he must die, his love of the Church is made stronger. Aged, bludgeoned, almost asleep, the Church speaks with sorrow, with the pain of great loss, with resignation to the prevailing season, still offering vital encouragement to the poet.

Line 14. "which thou must leave ere long." A memento mori.

Unconventionally, boldly, Shakespeare has made himself the addressee of the sonnet. It is he who sees the fading sun, who can no longer hear the song of the birds, who observes the consuming fire of martyrdom, and who must die himself. His love of the dying not dead Church does not die.

9. A Dozen To The Church

Imagine a human being who would instruct you in the moral life, telling you what's right and what's wrong and who, if you failed to follow the instructions, would forgive you if you were sorry for your transgression of the rules, promising to do penance. A child might see a parent as such a being. Would an adult, even if intoxicated by sexual passion, be apt to conceive of his lover in these terms? The question is pertinent as we look at the sonnets about to be considered.

None of them name an addressee, male or female. They are not to Jesuits nor to the poet's soul. They are not soliloquies. The addressee has to be figured out from what is said.

The Psalms set the pattern for verse addressed to God. The tradition had a Christian continuation:

> Recordare, Jesa pie,
>
> Quod sum causa viae tuae
>
> *Dies isue*

In English:

> Recall, sweet Jesus,
>
> That I am the reason for your way

Among the Italian masters of the sonnet Michelangelo spoke to Jesus in this way in a poem published in Venice in 1564:

> Ché ben c'alle promesse tua ś attenda,
>
> sperar forse, Signore, è troppo ardire
>
> c' ogni superchio indugio amor perdoni.

Ma pur par nel tuo sangue si compreda,

se per noi par non ebbe il tuo martire,

senza miisura sien tuo car domi.

In English

Although we note your promises,

Lord, it's perhaps too daring to hope

That love will pardon each super-delay.

But in your blood we comprehend

That, as your suffering for us had no equal,

Your dear gifts are without measure.

Michelangelo, p. 489.

God, Christ, the Church are addressees alternative to the usual addressees of the Sonnets. Since a number of poems from Sonnet 18 through Sonnet 126 are to a man, it could be presumed that the sonnets here that fall within that range are to a man. Similarly, Sonnet 143, which falls within the sequence where many sonnets address a woman, could be presumptively classed with those in the same sequence. Presumptions put an end to the puzzle, except that they do not identify the particular man or woman.

A more serious difficulty for the conventional view: If these poems are actually addressed to particular human beings, the poet – a practicing playwright, an astute businessman, an extraordinary interpreter of the human heart – has lapsed into childhood. He is addressing a beloved as if the poet was so besotted by lust that he thinks him or her to be his parent. Is that possible? Perhaps. Is it plausible? Not very. Is it likely? No. One's judgment here depends in part on one's estimate of Shakespeare, in part on one's experience of life, and in part on attention to the text. I argue – I cannot demonstrate – that, all things considered, the addressee in each of these sonnets is the Church.

The context of these sonnets is furnished by the Counter-Reformation's emphasis on the Church. At the start of what became the Reformation, Pope Leo X had identified as a principle of the Reformers: "It is certain that it is not in the power of the Church to determine the articles of faith, still less the laws of morals or of good works." The proposition was condemned in the militant bull *Exsurge, Domine*, June 15, 1520. *Denzinger*, No. 767. The Council of Trent in its fourth session, April 8, 1546, decreed that "no one should rely on his own judgment in matters of faith and morals, which pertain to the building of Christian doctrine." *Id.* no. 786. Maintaining the monopoly of the Church in teaching what was right and what was wrong, the Council also held out hope for the sinner – "a second plank after shipwreck" as the Council put it in the seventh session, June 17, 1546. What was required of the sinner was to stop sinning; a contrite and humble heart; confession of the sins; asking of absolution from the priest; and satisfaction by penance. *Id.* no. 867. As St. Thomas had taught, God alone could forgive sins, but the priests of the Church acted in God's name. *St. Thomas, Summa* III, q.84. Instructing, absolving, restoring to grace, the Church, acting by priests, was central.

The Church is "the most true mother of Christians," St. Augustine had said in his tract against the Manichees. *Augustine, De moribus*, p.62. In Sonnet 143, Mother Church is metaphorically invoked. In all of these sonnets a spiritual mentor is held in mind – not a bureaucratic institution as some today might think of an ecclesiastical structure, but a kind as well as vigilant guardian. "Charity requires," St. Thomas wrote explaining the sacrament of penance, "that a man grieve over an offense against a friend." *St. Thomas, Summa III, q.84, art.5.* After the absolution of the sin, penance is still necessary to restore health, "just as bodily medicine is necessary after a man falls into a dangerous disease." *Ibid.* The combination of powers – to prescribe what is right in conduct and belief; to forgive failure; and to exact penance – belonged to the Catholic Church as understood by her communicants. Only idolatrous parody would place these powers in a human.

These sonnets invite comparison with a more ambiguous sonnet of John Donne reflecting on the state of the Church, the bride of Christ:

> Show me deare Christ, thy Spouse, so bright and cleare.
> What is She, which on the other Shore
> Goes richly painted? Or which rob'd and tore
> Laments and mornes in Germany and here?
> Sleepes She a thousand, then peepes vp one yeare?
> Is She selfe truth and errs? now new, now' outwore?
> Doth She, 'and did She, and shall She evermore
> On one, on Severn, or on no hill appeare?
> Swells She with vs, or like adventuring knights
> First trauaile we to seeke and then make Love?
> Betray kind husband thy Spouse to our Sights,
> And let myne amorous Soule court thy mild Dove,
> Who is most trew, and pleasing to thee, then
> When She'is embrac'd and open to most Men.
>
> Donne, *Holy Sonnets*, p.19.

Commentators agree that "rob'd" = "robbed" and "tore" = "torn" and that "here" must be England. In England the only church that has been robbed and torn is the Catholic Church. Yet the poet is not certain where the true Church is. His last lines suggest an ecumenical embrace. The date of the sonnet is unknown. It was not published in seventeenth century editions of the *Holy Sonnets*, but was discovered and published by Edward Gosse in 1899. *Id*. 73. Donne does not speak to the Spouse. Like Shakespeare he treats her as a person.

Sonnet 74
"But be contented when that fell arrest"

But be contented when that fell arrest
Without all bail shall carry me away,
My life hath in this line some interest,
Which for memorial still with thee shall stay.
When thou reviewest this, thou dost review
The very part was consecrate to thee.
The earth can have but earth, which is his due;
My spirit is thine, the better part of me.
So then thou hast but lost the dregs of life,
The prey of worms, my body being dead;
The coward conquest of a wretch's knife,
Too base of thee to be rememb'red.
The worth of that is that which it contains,
And that is this, and this with thee remains.

Sonnet 73, on Booth's reading, ends with a couplet spoken by the poet to the beloved; Sonnet 74 begins with the poet speaking of himself. On this reading, the death anticipated in 73 is that of the beloved; the death expected in 74 is that of the poet. In contrast, in the reading I've proposed, the continuity consists in the poet in 74 addressing the dying Church of 73. That this reading is preferable is confirmed by the problems with a simple romantic reading of 74. The opening metaphor of fell arrest without bail; the language from the burial service, the consecration of what remains – all of these allusions invite associations that are not romantic or sexual.

The poet's death has been predicted by the Church in 73. In the opening lines of 74, the poet analogizes that death to the fate awaiting any resistence by the Church to the establishment. *Booth* 261 glosses "without all bail" by a reference to "without bail" in the statute of 1558 establishing "the Uniformity of Common Prayer." The arrest is a metaphor for death but not every arrest or death would be described as "fell", that is, cruel, painful, ruthless. *Booth* 260. The choice of "fell" emphasizes what a believer would have seen in death imposed by the state to suppress his faith.

The poet goes on to venture that in "this line" he has an "interest" that is, a share or part. *Booth* 261 thinks that "line" means "lines of verse"; he concedes that "these lines" might be "clearer." *Id.* His reading seems forced. Could "this line" be that of the martyrs? After the consecration of the bread and wine, there follows in the mass the remembrance of the dead and a prayer that God grant to the living "some part and fellowship" (*partem aliquam et societatem*) "with the holy apostles and martyrs." So the sonnet may be read to affirm the poet's part in the line of martyrs. An expert on recusancy literature goes further in detecting a pun on Anne Line. *Kilroy Letter.* Her kind of death, line 4 says, will have its memorial in the Church.

The poet's body will be buried with Christian rites: "Earth to earth, ashes to ashes, dust to dust" as the burial service prescribes. *Booth* 262. What will remain is his spirit "consecrate" to his addressee, the Church. Booth concedes that, "the metaphoric use of 'consecrate' establishes a religious reference." No doubt. But that the use is metaphoric is an undefended assumption. Booth notes the echo of the Christian ritual and calls the poem "a secular parody" but not a sacrilegious one; it is merely "a hyperbolic metaphor." *Id.* Is hyperbolic employment of religious ritual for the dead not a sacrilege? Was the poet's relation to a particular beloved as Platonic and unbodied as Booth here suggests? As a continuation of 73, Sonnet 74 responds to the dying Church: "I, too, may die as the line of martyrs have died. My spirit will live in you."

Before the Church the poet presents himself as a penitent:

Sonnet 111.
"O! for my sake do you wish fortune chide"

O! for my sake do you wish fortune chide,
The guilty goddess of my harmful deeds,
That did not better for my life provide
Than public means which public manners breeds.
Thence comes it that my name receives a brand,
And almost thence my nature is subdu'd
To what it works in, like the Dyer's hand:
Pity me, then, and wish I were renew'd;
Whilst, like a willing patient, I will drink,
Potions of Eisel 'gainst my strong infection;
No bitterness that I will bitter think,
Nor double penance to correct correction.
Pity me then, dear friend, and I assure ye,
Even that your pity is enough to cure me.

Sonnet 112.
"Your love and pity doth the impression fill"

Your love and pity doth the impression fill,
Which vulgar scandal stamp'd upon my brow;
For what care I who calls me well or ill,
So you o'er-green my bad, my good allow?
You are my All the world, and I must strive
To know my shames and praises from your tongue;
None else to me, nor I to none alive,
That my steel'd sense or changes right or wrong.
In so profound Abysm I throw all care
Of others' voices, that my Adder's sense
To critic and to flatterer stopped are.
Mark how with my neglect I do dispense:
You are so strongly in my purpose bred,
That all the world besides me thinks y'are dead.

Sonnet 111, "O for my sake do you wish fortune chide," casts back
a look at one aspect of the poet's life that led him astray. Fortune has
been "the guilty goddess" of his harmful course: "provide" in line 3
implicitly contrasts this goddess with Divine Providence. The poet
depended on the support of the public; so he accepted the morals of his
audience ("public manners"), so much that his reputation was injured
("received a brand") and his character reduced to the make-believe

medium in which he worked, as a glovemaker's hands get grimy in their work.

The poet asks for pity and asserts his willingness to accept medicinal measures ("potions of eisel", i.e., vinegar), to even do "double penance" to reform and more than reform himself – a hyperbole. The last two lines twice refer to the mercy – the pardon the Church offers the penitent – already asked for in line 8. The Church is addressed as "dear friend." Her mercy is enough to make him whole. The renewal he seeks in line 8 is absolution, which wipes out sin and creates a new man. As Booth acknowledges, line 8 is "a prayerful line" with "overtones of spiritual renewal" and Booth cites 2 Corinthians 4:16, Romans 12:2 and Titus 3:5. *Booth* 361.

Would the Church be addressed as "dear friend," as my interpretation holds? Book Four of *The Imitation of Christ* speaks to God of his "friendly invitation" (*amiabilis invitatio*). The *Dies irae*, as already noted, boldly reminds the judge:

> Recordare, Jesu pie,
>
> Quod sum causa tuae viae

The devotional heritage encouraged prayer cast as speech to a friend.

Despite his acknowledgment of scriptural resonances, Booth reads Sonnet 111 as a poem of human love because it is "linked" to Sonnet 110 by "similar subject matters," likenesses of minor detail and wit, and possibly by use of medical metaphor. His arguments are persuasive but not to the purpose he intends. I argue, *infra*, Chapter 10, that Sonnet 110 is addressed to the Virgin Mother of God. Linkage does exist between an address to this mother and an address to the Body of Christ. I acknowledge that much said to Mary could equally be said to the Church. It is a close call whether Sonnet 110 should not be classified with the other poems to the Church; but, for the reasons set out below, I see Sonnet 110 as primarily expressing Marian devotion.

The elements of the sacrament of penance are stated by characters in Shakespeare's plays as early as *Two Gentlemen of Verona* and as late as *The Winter's Tale*. *Beauregard* § 3. His familiarity with the elements is established. What is to be determined is whether, in this sonnet, the poet uses them figuratively or in their sacramental sense.

Read as love poetry to an individual, the apology in Sonnet 111 for what the poet's art has made him may be comprehensible by supposing that the love object of Sonnet 111 is a person of high status. But is the poet promising to reform by giving up acting or playwriting? The desire for reform, the acceptance of penance and the confident trust in the love that will forgive him present the poet not as fickle in affection for a desired male but as one acknowledging actual sins, partly accounted for by his trade, and wholly to be forgiven by the abundant love channeled through the Church.

Sonnet 112, "Your love and pity doth the impression fill," repeats the theme. Branded in Sonnet 111 by his work as a playwright, he again asserts that his public reputation has suffered; he has been sharply criticized, not for his plays, but for his conduct. What his reputation is does not bother him if the Church pardons him ("o'er green my bad, my good allow"). "o'er green" is coined by Shakespeare. *Booth* 363. It conveys a sense of transforming action, as grass or a plant transforms dirt. The Church is All his world; from her he learns what is praiseworthy and what is shameful. Only to the Church is he alive to alter his sense of what is right or wrong. He is as deaf as the proverbial adder to other critics and flatterers. In the profound depths of the Church he has put his trust. His present strong protestations may now serve as dispensation or excuse for his previous disregard of the Church.

When the poet writes in this way of the one who instructs him in right and wrong, he writes of instruction central to any human being, a fortiori to a poet. As Wallace Stevens has put it: "in every faithful poet the faithful poem is an act of conscience." *Stevens* 253. One could speculate that Shakespeare has turned his conscience over to another human being, but such a speculation deprives his conscience of its home. Shakespeare, as his writing repeatedly testifies, is profoundly aware of the centrality of conscience. To instruct conscience is not to surrender to the whims of a love object, but to get guidance from an identifiable guardian of morals.

The final two lines are Shakespearean hyperbole at its strongest. Everyone but he thinks the Church is dead, just as Truth and Beauty are thought dead in the *Loves Martyr* poem. Line 14 conveys the loneliness of the poet's position. Line 13 explains why he is in this isolated spot. It is because he identifies the Church with his own need that he has ended as the solitary soul clinging to belief in her existence. The Church is necessary if he is to obtain the pity he seeks. "[T]o my purpose bent" = "cherished in my intention," as *Booth* 364 suggests. When the adverb "strongly" is taken into account, the entire phrase is causative; it explains why the poet alone believes the Church lives. He cherishes the Church so intensely in intention that he thinks alive what everyone else has written off. The couplet is phrased in hyperbole to cap the declaration of his commitment to the Church as his only guide to what is right and what is wrong and the sole source of pardon. Of course, he is not literally alone in his faith, just as the Church is no more dead than Truth and Beauty are dead in the *Loves Martyr* poem. The poet exaggerates extravagantly to proclaim his love that finds life in what the world thinks extinct.

"besides", a word that functions as either an adverb or a preposition, is in line 14 a preposition governing "me". In this position, its meaning, well-established by the fourteenth century, is "other than". See *OED* at "besides". Other than the poet, the world believes the Church dead. A number of editors of the *Sonnets*, not understanding the reference, have boldly emended line 14 to read "That all the world besides methinks are dead." See *Booth* 368. This rewriting treats "besides" as an adverb and makes the line say that the poet thinks that the rest of the world other than the beloved is dead. No justification exists for remaking the text in this way.

Other efforts to amend line 14 – for example, to read "y" as an archaic form of "th'" – are considered and rejected by *Booth* 368-369. He himself considers the poem to be "incomprehensible." *Id.* He contends that Sonnet 112 is an "unfinished poem or one that Shakespeare abandoned in frustration." *Id.* 369. Line 8 "does not in fact deliver meaning". *Id.* 366. Line 14 is "more grossly faulty", because it is not related to the thirteen preceding lines. *Id.* 368. The apparently idolatrous rhetoric is read as the hyperbole of romance and as artistic slush.

This approach leads to Booth's mystification as to the meaning of line 8, which expresses the poet's commitment to the Church's judgment. It leads to line 14 being incomprehensible when related to what precedes it. Abandoned, incomprehensible, meaningless the poem is hopeless. Writing it off, the critic fails to ask the critical questions: Who has power to "o'er green his bad", i.e., make the poet new, except the Church? Why would even a particular friend have the power to instruct the poet's conscience, to tell him what is right and what is wrong? Why would the world suppose that the poet's particular friend was dead?

I go on to four more poems that express repentance and the poet's love of the Church:

Sonnet 115.
"Those lines that I before have writ do lie"

Those lines that I before have writ do lie,
Even those that said I could not love you dearer:
Yet then my judgment knew no reason why
My most full flame should afterwards burn clearer.
But reckoning Time, whose million'd accidents
Creep in 'twixt vows, and change decrees of Kings,
Tan sacred beauty, blunt the sharp'st intents,
Divert strong minds to the course of altering things:
Alas! why fearing of time's tyranny,
Might I not then say, now I love you best,
When I was certain o'er incertainty,
Crowning the present, doubting of the rest:
Love is a Babe, then might I not say so,
To give full growth to that which still doth grow.

Sonnet 116. "Let me not to the marriage of true minds"

Let me not to the marriage of true minds
Admit impediments. Love is not love
Which alters when it alteration finds,
Or bends with the remover to remove.
O, no, it is an ever-fixed mark
That looks on tempests and is never shaken;
It is the star to every wandering bark,
Whose worth's unknown, although his height be taken.
Love's not Time's fool, though rosy lips and cheeks
Within his bending sickle's compass come.
Love alters not with his brief hours and weeks,
But bears it out even to the edge of doom.
If this be error and upon me prov'd,
I never writ, nor no man ever lov'd.

Sonnet 117.
"Accuse me thus, that I have scanted all"

Accuse me thus, that I have scanted all
Wherein I should your great deserts repay,
Forgot upon your dearest love to call,
Whereto all bonds do tie me day by day;
That I have frequent been with unknown minds,
And given to time your own dear purchas'd right;
That I have hoisted sail to all the winds
Which should transport me farthest from your sight.
Book both my wilfulness and errors down,
And on just proof surmise, accumulate,
Bring me within the level of your frown,
But shoot not at me in your waken'd hate,
Since my appeal says I did strive to prove
The constancy and virtue of your love.

Sonnet 119.
"What potions have I drunk of Siren tears"

What potions have I drunk of Siren tears,
Distill'd from Limbecks foul as hell within,
Applying fears to hopes, and hopes to fears,
Still losing when I saw myself to win!
What wretched errors hath my heart committed,
Whilst it hath thought itself so blessed never?
How have mine eyes out of their Spheres been fitted
In the distraction of this madding fever!
O benefit of ill, now I find true
That better is by evil still made better;
And ruin'd love when it is built anew
Grows fairer than at first, more strong, far greater.
So I return rebuk'd to my content,
And gain by ills thrice more than I have spent.

Sonnets 113 and 114 could be construed to continue the sequence of Sonnets 111-112. They are sufficiently ambiguous that the argument from proximity is not enough to decide the meaning. I skip them and turn to Sonnet 115, "Those lines that I before have writ do lie." The poet has written of his "love" of the addressee before but his judgment was that this love, heartfelt as it was, would not become "clearer", that is, more certain. The first quatrain sets the stage on which the final couplet will triumphantly conclude.

The second quatrain is an apparent digression.   Vows can be sapped by time, just as with time one royal decision may be supplanted by another.   The chance events (the "millioned accidents") that occur in the course of time also blacken beauty that is sacred, frustrate well-framed purposes and turn even strong minds.   What is the relevance of these observations to the opening theme?   A critic committed to the belief that here Shakespeare is writing love poetry finds no relevance at all: "the sense of the poem is entirely complete without Q2." *Vendler* 484.   The digression, however, is only apparent, the relevance is striking, if it is the Church that is addressed.   It would seem that this possibility is worth pursuing. It is almost unbelievable that Shakespeare would waste four out of fourteen lines.

Quatrain 2's references are not random nor are they "philosophical commonplaces" as *Booth* 385 characterizes them.   When the Church is accepted as the addressee, the second quatrain reads as a discreet reminder of the disasters that have befallen her.   Vows – most significantly the monarch's coronation oath to guard the Church – have been broken; by royal decree the Church has been outlawed. The Church's beauty has been blackened. Supporters of the Church have found their plans defeated.   Persons resolute in their religion have been turned "to the course of alt'ring things". Line 8 is a pun: the activity these persons engage in is changing things or altering altars. The allusion may be specifically to John Shakespeare altering the altar in Stratford or it may be a broader reference to all the alterations made by the new establishment.

Having noted the ravages in religion that have taken place as time has gone on, and acknowledging that most things do change with time ("time's tyranny"), the poet fears that nothing is permanent. He turns to his own love of the Church. He has now reached certainty where before he was uncertain. Why should he not say right now that he loves the Church best? In that declaration he would be "[c]rowning the present." Q line 10 introduces with a colon the point of the poem. The poet's hesitation had a reason. It is that love itself changes. But it changes differently than what is affected by the "millioned accidents". Love grows. Why should it grow? Because it is a baby. Like a baby "it still doth grow."

"Babe" makes *Booth* 383 think of Cupid. But Cupid doesn't grow. This Babe is different. "Babe" is capitalized in Q, although not by modern editors nor in Q when the word is employed in Sonnet 143. I follow Q: Demonstration cannot be based on the printer's choice of a capital. But neither should the possibility be ignored that the author spoke of "a Babe" and intended an allusion. Shakespeare most probably knew "The burning Babe" of Robert Southwell. This poem comes to mind in Shakespeare's use of "Babe." In Southwell, Christ on Christmas Day appears as a baby in flames of which

> Love is the fire . . . .
> "The burning Babe,"
> *St. Robert,* p. 14.

The love incarnate in the Babe will grow. Shakespeare had at hand no stronger instance of incandescent and increasing love.

Booth comments: "Shakespeare's Sonnet 115 can be described as deriving its energy from a sustained quibble on 'perfect' in its literal sense ('complete', 'incapable of augmentation') and 'perfect' less precisely used to mean 'most excellent'." *Booth* 379. Booth's exegesis is eccentric. The word "perfect" is not employed in the poem. More fundamentally, a quibble will not sustain a sonnet.

Sonnet 116, "Let me not to the marriage of true minds" introduces another metaphor – a religious metaphor as old as the Epistle to the Ephesians' comparison of Christ's love of the Church to a husband's love of his wife. Ephesians 5:21-32. Like many, I have read this poem as, in part, a celebration of married love. On reflection, and after experience, I find the marriage of minds, even if understood as synecdoche, to be a misleading way of speaking of human matrimony. I propose treating the marriage of minds as an analogy.

Familiar with the biblical analogy central to Ephesians, Christian theologians had created a second analogy. The mutual love of Christ and the Church was paralleled by the mystical mutual love of God and the individual human soul. Knowing the biblical example and probably aware of the mystical one, Shakespeare has created a third analogue to the love of Christ and the Church. It is the mutual love of the Church and the believer. This union of minds may be suggested by St. Paul's claim:

> But we have the mynd of Christe
>
> 1 Corinthians 2:16.

The qualification of the minds as "true" introduces the theological theme of truth. The opening two lines, employing the canonical term "impediment," are framed as a prayer that to this loving union no obstacle be placed. A meditation follows on what this love requires.

Lines 2-4 declare that such love rises above alterations. The pun of Sonnet 115 is repeated and made more pointed by reference to "the remover," i.e., the one who effects the alterations, the whitewasher of the saints' paintings, the iconoclast. The poem continues with celebration of the strength of this love. The paean affirms the truth of St. Paul: Love "[s]uffereth all things, believeth all things, hopeth all things, endureth all things." 1 Corinthians 13:7. As now put by the poet, love is "an ever-fixed mark" for barks whose uncertain course is implicitly contrasted with that of the bark of Peter.

"Tempest" functions like "show'rs" in Sonnet 124, *infra* to designate bouts of persecution. "Storms" was a metaphor that Garnet writing Aquaviva employed in the same way. *Caraman* 228. Southwell used "bloody showers" to describe Herod's slaughter of the babies of Bethlehem. *St. Robert*, p. 9. The paradigmatic tempest was, of course, the storm on the Sea of Galilee. In the language of the Geneva Bible, often used by Shakespeare, "Behold there arose a great tempest in the sea in so much of the ship was covered with waters," while Jesus slept. The disciples woke him up. And Jesus "rebuked the windes and the waves and stilled the storm." Mark 8:24-26.

For bad weather to stand for the action of government persecutors does not appear to be unusual metonymy. Its very ordinariness make it difficult to be sure that what is being referred to is anything but a general sense of oppression. "Tempest," as it functions as the title of the play, makes bad weather a general stand-in for troubles. But the weather metaphor can be read more narrowly. Just as "stormy weather" in a popular song of the twentieth century signified romantic difficulties, so the weather metaphor may have worked for the Catholic community to indicate the repressive movements of the government. These outbursts against the Church are storms that pass. Love shines like a star to guide those wandering in error.

Throughout the poem the love personified is the bond between believer and the Church. This love occupies a lofty site ("height"), but its depth ("worth") has not been plumbed. I gladly accept Booth's suggestion that what is echoed here is Ephesians' reference to "the unsearchable riches of Christ," which is coupled in the epistle with the prayer that converts to Christianity be able to comprehend "what is the breadth, and length, and depth, and height, and to know the love of Christ, which passeth knowledge." Ephesians 3:17-19.

"Love's not Time's fool." The line brings to mind the dying Hotspur's declaration in *Henry IV*, Part J, 5.4.80, which speaks of "life, time's fool." Love, unlike life, is stronger than time. In Ephesians, traditionally attributed to St. Paul, the writer prays that you will "not be as fooles, but as wise, redeeming the time." Ephesians 5:15-16. Accepting this biblical allusion, one finds that "time's fools" in this context carries a different meaning from "the fools of time" in Sonnet 124; here it is not innocence but lack of wisdom that is stressed in comparison to the redeeming action of love. Love lasts though the lovers age. The third quatrain culminates in the statement that love "bears it out ev'n to the edge of doom." By "doom" the Day of Judgment is meant, the day when this world ends and every person is judged by God. Love lasts to the last reckoning.

The final couplet is an emphatic assertion of the truth of what the poet has just said. A theological term, error, is employed to set up a reductio ad absurdum. It would be as bad a mistake to deny the mutual love of Church and Christian as to deny that Shakespeare ever wrote or that anyone ever loved. The absurdity is double. It would be tantamount to denying the poet's personal history. It would be tantamount to denying the universal experience of humankind.

Three misinterpretations:

(1) "One means of achieving universality and vividness at once is bombast, high-sounding, energetic nonsense . . . , much of [the poem's] strength and value is of the same sort that bombast has. Sonnet 116 achieves effective definition unlimited by any sense of effective limitation." *Booth* 387.

(2) An "undercurrent of frivolous sexual suggestiveness" runs through the poem. Its metaphors and ideas "seem just on the point of veering off toward puerile joking about temporary male impotence – loss of tumescence – after sexual climax." *Id.* 391. A "substratum of random bisexual reference" suggests "preposterous teasing." *Id.* 392.

(3) Sonnet 116 is rebuttal of a previous and unexpected declaration "by the young man" that love does alter. *Vendler* 488, noting

that "no reader" has ever read the poem's opening this way. *Id*. 491. The novelty of Vendler's claim is not an objection. The unlikeliness of the supposition that Ephesians is unrolled to do battle with an imaginary declaration by the imagined male is.

Booth's two comments are equally unpersuasive. To find sly sexual innuendo, not openly expressed, but making up a "substratum" of meaning is to subordinate the text to the critic's projections. To find the poem a species of bombast is to treat unseriously the allusions to St. Paul, the reference to the time of Judgment, and the emphatic contrast between error and truth. To suppose that this poem, suffused with allusions to the writing of St. Paul, playing on the difference between true minds and error, and measuring love's lastingness to the time of Judgment, is the expression of affection for a particular human individual is to ignore the weight of the evidence and the extraordinary emphasis on personal and universal experience in the reductio ad absurdum.

That the scriptural references, when read in a secular sense, become bombast is evidence enough, one might think, that the secular reading is suspect. Taken on their own terms – the terms of Christian tradition – the lines express exquisitely the deepest kind of love. Once understood and read by me as an epithalamium, Sonnet 116 now speaks to me in that language of truth and error appropriate not to the expression of marital affection but to celebration of spiritual combat.

Sonnet 117, "Accuse me this that I have scanted all" combines celebration of the Church with a quasi-apology for the poet's conduct in relation to the Church. He is willing to accept as deserved rebuke that he has neglected his obligation to reciprocate the Church's goodness and has even gone so far as not to seek the

Church's help (lines 2-4). Even worse, he has strayed doctrinally ("been with unknown minds"); he has been a time-server, yielding under the pressures of the moment what is owed to the Church ("your own dear purchased right"). The right is dearly bought, the subtext runs, because bought by the blood of the Lord. There is also a pun. The Church's rite, i.e., the mass, has been purchased by the sacrifice of Christ. The poet has wasted ("given to time") this costly benefit. His doctrinal deviations have been many ("sailed to all the winds") and taken him very far from the Church. He is willing that the Church note both his wilfulness and the theological errors he has entertained. The poet acknowledges the Church's right to call him to account and manifest displeasure at his conduct, but he asks not to be utterly rejected ("shoot not at me"). The poet has filed an appeal, a term of canon law, current among Catholics in 1600 when dissidents filed an appeal against the appointment of the archpriest. Here "appeal" is used metaphorically to designate Shakespeare's defense: he was proving the steadiness and strength of the Church's love; "prove" in line 13 operates as a perfect pun; meaning both "to test" and "to demonstrate." The poet was testing, i.e., pushing to the limit the Church's willingness to forgive. He was also demonstrating how far this forgiveness would go.

Booth 392 remarks on the thematic connections of this sonnet to its immediate predecessor. Were it not for this connection and for the references to "unknown minds," "your right," and "appeal," the identity of the addressee might be set down as uncertain. The thematic topics tie 117 to 116 and require 117's interpretation in the same spiritual way.

<u>Misinterpretation</u>. Sonnet 117 is a rebuttal of accusations by "the young man" who is the object of the speaker's love. Both 116 and 117 involve "an exposure of the young man's ignoble nature." *Vendler* 495.

So the poet's confession is recast as a set of unfair complaints by the imagined youth, who is further scored for "vulgarity of diction" because phrases like "hoisted sails to all the winds" are now attributed to his list of imagined accusations, rather than seen as part of the poet's humble acknowledgment of his errors.

An argument could be advanced for reading Sonnet 118 as related to 117, but the metaphors in it are too clogged to permit a convincing exegesis. I skip it and go on to Sonnet 119, "What potions have I drunk of Siren tears." The poem expresses, with a new set of metaphors, the poet's revulsion from his past sins. Just as he thought the new remedies would cure an imagined sickness, so he imagined himself "so blessed never" at the very time he had fallen into error – again the term has a theological connotation. His ruin has now been repaired. His love is now greater because of his fall and repentance.

Southwell had brought "tears" and "tunes" together. Commemorating the Massacre of the Innocents, he had written, "Your tunes are teares." "The flight into Egypt," *St. Robert*, p. 9. In Southwell's *St. Peters Complaint* 1.311, the repentant Peter, who has denied the Lord, declares that he has been seduced by "syrens sugred tunes," a simple variation of the expression "siren songs," while "syren" designates anything tempting one to sin. Shakespeare brings "siren" and "tears" into conjunction to express what yielding to temptation means: the sinner is beguiled by the music meant to tease and trap him, the result is tears, hence "siren tears."

Line 7 recalls Oberon's speech in *A Midsummer Night's Dream* that describes the rebel earls as moving "out of their spheres": so, too, the poet's eyes rebelled. Line 11's reference to "ruined love" is matched in Sonnet 125 where the poet's "great bases for eternity" are subject to ruining. Over all, the poem celebrates the good that has come of his bad. That, one might say, is putting a bold face on what he now sees as evil. The precedent lies in the liturgy for Easter: Adam's sin becomes his *felix culpa* or "fortunate fault." *Booth* 404. From his primal misdeed has arisen the redemption of humankind by Christ; so, line 14, asserts "[I] gain by ills thrice more than I have spent."

Despite noting the allusion to Adam's *felix culpa*, Booth maintains that the sonnet sustains a sexual note. Lines 1 and 2 are "suggestive of perverse sexual activity." *Booth* 400. He offers the information that, in classical mythology, sirens are female, but that "siren" as an adjective does not necessarily imply a reference to women. He goes on to observe that alembics (the "limbecks" of line 2) have a shape and interrelation of parts that make "obvious" a suggestion of homosexual fellatio. This athletic anatomy of a bottle is ingenious. It tells us nothing about "siren tears." It is difficult to believe that deliberate echoes of the Easter liturgy and of *St. Peters Complaint* and the reference to ruin that chimes with Sonnet 124 are all marshaled to express to one human lover the poet's disillusion with several other human lovers.

Other poems to the Church, not in any sequence, are sprinkled through the Sonnets:

Sonnet 31
"Thy bosom is endeared with all hearts"

Thy bosom is endeared with all hearts,
Which I by lacking have supposed dead;
And there reigns Love, and all Love's loving parts,
And all those friends which I thought buried.
How many a holy and obsequious tear
Hath dear religious love stol'n from mine eye,
As interest of the dead, which now appear
But things remov'd that hidden in there lie!
Thou art the grave where buried love doth live,
Hung with the trophies of my lovers gone,
Who all their parts of me to thee did give,
That due of many now is thine alone:
Their images I lov'd, I view in thee,
And thou (all they) hast all the all of me.

Sonnet 66.
"Tired with all these, for restful death I cry"

Tired with all these, for restful death I cry,
As to behold desert a beggar born,
And needy Nothing trimm'd in jollity,
And purest faith unhappily forsworn,
And gilded honour shamefully misplac'd,
And maiden virtue rudely strumpeted,
And right perfection wrongfully disgrac'd,
And strength by limping sway disabled,
And art made tongue-tied by authority,
And Folly (Doctor-like) controlling skill,
And simple-Truth miscall'd Simplicity,
And captive-good attending Captain ill:
Tir'd with all these, from these would I be gone,
Save that to die, I leave my love alone.

Sonnet 83.
"I never saw that you did painting need"

I Never saw that you did painting need,
And therefore to your fair no painting set;
I found (or thought I found) you did exceed
That barren tender of a Poet's debt:
And therefore have I slept in your report,
That you yourself, being extant, well might show
How far a modern quill doth come too short,
Speaking of worth, what worth in you doth grow.
This silence for my sin you did impute,
Which shall be most my glory, being dumb;
For I impair not beauty, being mute,
When others would give life, and bring a tomb.
There lives more life in one of your fair eyes
Than both your Poets can in praise devise.

Sonnet 31 may be read as a baroque valentine, "a love-compliment"
as *Vendler* 170-171 puts it. Religious language is put to romantic use. The
climax, *Booth* 184 declares, announces a conversion to "monotheism,"
i.e., the poet now worships only one man. So read, it's extravagant.
But Shakespeare is extravagant. The minor emendations made by the
critics – "thee" for "there" in line 8 and the uncapitalization of "love"
in line 3 – appear unremarkable.

On "my lovers," Booth has a cross reference to his discussion of "love" and "lovers" in Sonnet 126. He notes that in ordinary communications of the time the terms had as much sexual content as "Dear Sir" in a business letter today. On the other hand, context can make them sexual, and Sonnet 31 is such a context. *Booth* 432. If one rejects his reading of the context, "lovers" means "friends." That his friends have trophies suggests that they are martyrs.

It seems that a reading other than Booth's is possible, more in keeping with what Vendler acknowledges as "the somber tone" of the poem. Take the religious language and imagery at full face value. Follow where they point. "Thy bosom is endeared with all hearts," speaks to the Church as she exists in the faithful departed: the theme is announced in the first two lines. The poet, when he lacked faith, had thought his friends dead; now he see that they are like a church's images removed by the removers only to be securely hidden. In fact, they are alive, constituting the membership not of the Church militant but the membership of the Church suffering in Purgatory or the Church triumphant in heaven. The insistence on the number of persons the poet intends to commemorate is striking. No single individual is contemplated. "All" is the plural used to invoke the dead. "All" is employed in the first line and in the last line and in the fourth line to describe them. "Love" in Q is twice capitalized in line 3. In the realm in which these deceased friends live, Love rules. "And these reigns Love and all Love's loving parts": in heaven love is triumphant. "parts" = "qualities" as in *Much Ado About Nothing* V, II, 54.

Love may be understood as the mutual charity of these souls or it can be read as meaning God as, in the First Letter of John, God is love. Possibly the printer of the Quarto edition read it the second way when he twice capitalized love. But I do not rely on this possibility: capitalization in the seventeenth century was arbitrary. What I do maintain is that not every mention of love in the Sonnets should be taken to mean the love of two human beings for each other. In this sonnet, the multitude invoked by Line 1, the acknowledgment in Line 2 that the poet once believed that these friends were dead, and the earthily explicit "buried" show that Shakespeare is not thinking of any living individual. The poet had mourned the loss of the departed with religious submission ("holy and obsequious tear") and wept "with dear religious love." He had paid, as it were, interest on the grief created by their deaths. Now, his faith regained, he sees that they lie there (so in Q), that is, within the Church's bosom. This bosom, paradoxically called "the grave," is where they rest. This grave is festooned with "the trophies of my lovers gone" – that is, the friends who have died have departed with the symbols of their victory over death, just as the wheel, the ax, and the grill were the trophies of earlier martyred saints. The deceased friends have carried with them parts of the poet himself: what he owed to all these friends is now surrendered by them to the Church alone. What the poet had loved in his friends ("their images") came from the Church, constituted by "all they," and to the Church he gives himself. The Church in whom his friends live has what he gave them and he now gives the rest of himself. The "all the all of me" is assertive, comprehensive, and itself triumphant.

Booth 184 says of line 7 of Sonnet 31: "the dead, which now appear" are in "their momentarily apparent resurrection." For him their resurrection is only apparent. Determinedly, he reads the poem for sexual references. The mention of "things" in line 8, he suggests, means penises. With a cross-reference to his page 146, he suggests that "parts" in line 11 can mean sex organs. *Id*. 183. He maintains "due " in line 12 is a pun for "dew," apparently from an ejaculation. Booth then retreats, saying that the sexual allusions are "unexploited." *Id*. An unexploited pun sounds as though the double meaning was his discovery. Have the puns remained so long unexploited? None of these possible puns sits very well with the "holy and obsequious tear" of line 5 or the "dear religious love" of line 6 or explains much of the poem

Sonnet 31 is preceded by Sonnet 30, "When to the sessions of sweet silent thought" lamenting "precious friends lost in death's dateless night." It is tempting to read the two sonnets together and to see the concluding couplet of Sonnet 30 as an introduction to Sonnet 31:

> But if the while I think on thee, dear friend,
>
> All losses are restored, and sorrows end

The friends of Sonnet 30 are not metaphorically dead. They are held in dateless night. The linkage of 30 to 31 suggests that is true of the friends of 31. On this reading, "dear friend" refers to the Church in whom the lost friends are restored. But, taken by itself, Sonnet 30 may be restricted to an individual human figure.

Sonnet 66, "Tired with all these for restful death I cry" is far from triumphant. It is not clearly addressed to anyone. The implicit addressee is "my love" to whom Line 14 gives prominence. Read by itself, "my love" could easily be taken to mean an individual. The content of the poem makes such a reading unlikely. What have the enumerated disasters to do with a particular person? Why is the mocking of Truth nearly the climatic ill? It is my contention that the multitude of evils set out are things seen as especially evil by the community of which Shakespeare formed a part. Cataloguing them leads to near-despair except for his religious commitment.

Booth supplies no historical context nor reason why the poet lists the evils enumerated. If one takes into account Shakespeare's relation to the recusants of the *Loves Martyr* poem, every line reflects the misery of his London associates. The poem is a cri de coeur. Merit is unrewarded. Nobodies thrive. Oaths are broken. Honor is forgotten.

Women are prostituted. The perfect oblation of the mass ("right" or "rite" perfection) is wrongfully dishonored. The strong are ruled by the crippled. Authority silences art as ruffians removed the tongue of Lavinia in *Titus Andronicus*. Fools rule the wise. Folly, personified as in Erasmus, is "Doctor-like", i.e., like a theologian, in this instance an heretical theologian. The Truth (capitalized in Q) is mocked as simple-mindedness. The good is subordinated to the bad. The England of the poem is the England of the *Loves Martyr* poem: Truth and Beauty lie dead. What keeps the speaker going? His love, a love that in context is the Church.

The context may be tightened by consideration of the career and connections of Southwell. Admitted to the Society of Jesus in 1578, he was sent on the English mission in 1586, and executed in 1596. He was thirty-three at the time of his death. *Caraman* "Martyrs" 328. He was Shakespeare's senior by two years, a person of physical beauty, and an audacious priest and poet. Surprised and captured in June, 1592, he had been in residence in Uxbridge with the Bellamy family, Catholics who had already fallen under the government's suspicion. Anne, their oldest daughter, twenty-one, was already in prison; her father informed the Privy Council that she was there raped by Topcliffe. *Hogge* 177. A rapist may inflict such damage on his victim that she will fail "to escape or cry out for help when in a public place" because now lacking "sufficient ego-strength, self-confidence and will power" to escape the "complete domination" of the man who has her in his power. See *Pregerson, J.* at 605; *Williams,* 755-62. Anne, in fact, became dependent on Topcliffe and was turned into an informer, supplying information as to Southwell's whereabouts, his description, and his exact hiding place in the family house, so that when Topcliffe and his men raided the home, they scooped him up without difficulty. *Caraman* 148. Topcliffe produced Anne as a witness at Southwell's trial to testify that the Jesuit instructed her in equivocation. *Gerard* 269. Anne, pregnant, was forced to marry Nicholas Jones, a Topcliffe henchman, underkeeper of the Gate House prison, "my boye, Nicholas" as Topcliffe described him in a note to the Queen. *Brownlow* 2003, 172. Topcliffe's boy could scarcely have been suitable for a bride of the status of the Bellamys. *Id.*

It is impossible now to verify the story of Topcliffe's conduct with Anne, but it must have been current in the Catholic community. It was asserted in 1598 by Robert Barnes, a Catholic who, at his trial, was allowed to speak freely. *Devlin 276.* The betrayal of Southwell was the greatest disaster that the Jesuits in England suffered prior to Garnet's trial. Anne had been Topcliffe's prey. "Strumpeted" can mean "made a strumpet" or "falsely accused of being a strumpet." *Booth* 249. Given the evidence of Shakespeare's interest in Southwell's work, he could well have generalized the single shocking episode of his betrayal and referred to its background in Line 6: "And maiden virtue rudely strumpeted." How deeply the mild and moderate Garnet felt about Topcliffe is conveyed in his description of the man to Aquaviva: "*homo sordidissimus,*" the foulest of men. *Caraman* 107. Among London Catholics, Topcliffe was tops as "captain ill"; but the reference in Sonnet 66, on its face, is general. The raw injustice of Southwell's capture and Anne Bellamy's treatment cannot have been far from the poet's mind as he wrote.

Sonnet 83 "I never saw that you did painting need" is a puzzle. The first two lines declare that the poet has not "painted" the addressee before. The third and fourth lines announce that the addressee seems beyond a poet's power to paint. Therefore the poet has been silent. It is, I suggest, impossible to suppose that the "you" of these verses is the young man who is identified by conventional critics as the addressee or subject of at least one hundred and nine poems; silence from the poet has not been his fate. Yet in the first two quatrains the poet is gracefully explaining a silence of which he stands accused.

The eighth line provides one clue, the growing worth of the addressee. Could it be the Church nourished by the blood of martyrs? A "modern pen" may well come too short in celebrating an institution over 1,500 years old. The ninth line says Shakespeare has been accused of sin for being silent, as Southwell suggested in the poem "The Author to the Reader" that precedes the printed text of Southwell's poetry published in 1595. *Southwell, Poems* (1967) lvi. The twelfth line is mysterious if one doesn't go outside the poem: who are "the others" who "would give life" but "bring a tomb?" "Tomb" in line 12 could have been pronounced "tome", suggesting a volume of writing. *Booth* 283. Booth does not explain why the double meaning would be appropriate. But one may think of Southwell, who wrote poetry as well as prose to put the case of the Church in England and was then killed by the state. The "others" include him and those whose efforts to give life to the Church have ended in their execution. The phrase "fair eyes" treats the Church as a living person who, still beautiful, contemplates the course of events. Booth offers no explanation of this phrase nor of line 14's climactic reference to "both your poets." His blankness points to the puzzle's solution beyond his commentary. The final line, I believe, may contain the answer: "both your poets" may be Southwell and Shakespeare. Both are the Church's.

The Southwell-Shakespeare connection can be seen in a variety of texts. The hunted hare is an incidental figure in *Venus and Adonis*. This allegorical animal is sympathetically described. It can't be demonstrated but it is possible that he has been suggested by Southwell, himself a hunted hare, who had already written:

The feebles part puts up enforced wrong

And silent sees that speech could not amend

. . .

The tender larke will find a tyme to flye

And fearfull hare to runne a quiet race.

"Scorne not the Leaste," *St. Robert* 60.

Southwell's poetry was thoughtful – some might say didactic. It was imaginative – some might say fantastic. Compared to Shakespeare's, its range was narrow. But there was enough there to engage the younger man, in particular Southwell's attempts, through imagining the thoughts of characters in Scripture, to stimulate sluggish or half-skeptical English Catholics. In this apostolic endeavor there stand out "Christes Sleeping Friends," "St. Peters Complaint" and "Josephes Amazement". Each uses a figure in Scripture to convey a sense of the contemporary Catholic situation.

The sleeping friends appear to be a gentle comment on the inactive Catholics of England. The amazed Joseph can't quite believe that his wife has not slept with someone and can't quite believe that she has. With remarkably realistic candor the poem presents the puzzlement of a husband whose wife has mysteriously become pregnant. The theme was not original. A medieval mystery play was entitled *Joseph's Doubt*. But Southwell's pointed poem could be read to present the doubtful state of mind of English Catholics unsure if they were credulous fools to believe that their religion would ever be restored to its rightful place or blessed in believing that some kind of miracle would set everything right.

The theme of Southwell's poem on Peter focuses on Peter's three denials of Christ, followed by his bitter regret, and his ultimate pardon. At its start, "The Author to the Reader" addresses a contemporary:

The Author to the Reader of the poem.

Deare eie that daynest to let fall a looke,

On these sad memories of Peters plaintes:

Must not to see some mud in cleerest brooke,

They once were brittle mould, that now are Saintes.

Their weakenesses is no warrant to offend:

If equities even-hand the ballance held,

Where Peters sinnes and ours were made the weightes:

Ounce, for his Dramme: Pound, for his Ounce we yeeld:

His Ship would groane to feele some sinners freightes.

So ripe is vice, so greene is vertues bud:

The world doth waxe in evill, but waine in good.

This makes my mourning muse resolve in teares,

This Theames my heavy penne to plaine in prose.

Christes Thorne is sharpe, no head his Garland weares:

Still finest wits are stilling Venus Rose.

In Paynim toyes the sweetest vaines are spent:

To Christian workes, few have their tallents lent.

License my single penne to seeke a pheere,

You heavenly sparkes of wit, shew native light:

Cloude not with mistie loves your Orient cleere,

Sweete flightes you shoote; learne once to levell right.

Favour my wish, well wishing workes no ill:

I moove the Suite, The Graunt restes in your will.

St. Robert 63.

This dedication can be read as directed to a single reader among the wits "still stilling Venus Rose," Shakespeare's poem, *Venus and Adonis* was published in 1593. It was not in print when Southwell completed *St. Peters Complaint. Klause* 51. But Shakespeare's poem could have been in manuscript when Southwell wrote. "Will" may be encased in a pun in the last sentence in Southwell's introduction.

The introduction also expresses a desire for "a pheere," that is, "a companion." See *St. Robert* 164. Who better as a companion for a poet than Shakespeare? These considerations suggest but do not prove that Shakespeare was meant. Then take into account the prose passage that functions as a second preface to the edition of 1595. (Did a printer have two different introductions and use them both?). The prose preface comes first:

The Author to his loving Cosen

Poets by abusing their talent, and making the follies and fayninges of love, the customary subject of their base endeavors, have so discredited this facultie, that a Poet, a Lover, and a Liar, are reckoned by many three wordes of one signification. But the vanity of man cannot counterpoyse the authority of God, who delivering many partes of Scripture in verse, and by his Apostle willing us to exercise our devotion in Himmes and Spiritual Sonnets, waranteth the Art to be good, and the use allowable. . . . Christ himself by making a Himme, the conclusion of his last Supper, and the Prologue to the Pageant of his Passion, gave his Spouse a methode to immitate, as in the office of the Church it appeareth, and all men a paterne to know the true use of this measured and footed stile . . . . . Blame me not (good Cosen) though I send you a blame-worthy present, in which the most that can commend it, is the good will of the writer . . . If in mee this be a fault, you cannot be faultlesse that did importune mee to committe it, and therfore you must beare parte of the penance, when it shall please sharp censures to impose it. In the meane time with many good wishes I send you these few ditties, add you the Tunes, and let the Meane, I pray you, be still a part in all your Musike.

Southwell 1967 1-2.

The first printing of the words addressed to the Reader and those addressed to his loving Cousin occurred immediately upon Southwell's execution. *Id.* iv-vi. Over twenty years later an edition of the poems printed by the Jesuit press at Douai identified the loving cousin as "Master W.S." To find W.S. stands for our poet goes beyond the evidence. What does seem clear is that the loving cousin was a specific person, a poet who needed criticism and encouragement and a poet who encouraged Southwell to write his own poetry. If the prose preface is read together with the verses of "The Author to the Reader," it is not unreasonable to guess that this person is Shakespeare. It seems not too much to think that Shakespeare took up in the 1590's Southwell's suggestion that we "exercise our devotion in Himmes and Spiritual Sonnets".

Like other of Shakespeare's variations on a text before his eyes, the connection between what he read and what he wrote cannot be demonstrated. All that is possible is a judgment of probability influenced by observation of the author's other allusions. The first sentence of "The Author to his Loving Cosen" is inextricably tied to the trio in Theseus' speech:

> The lunatic, the lover, and the poet
> Are of imagination all compact.
>
> *A Midsummer Night's Dream* 5.1.8-9.

Like Oberon's reference to the mermaid on the dolphin's back, this combination of nouns meets no requirement of the play. It does seem to be a response to Southwell, all of whose poetry was written before his arrest in 1592. Although the date of composition of *Midsummer* is not known, it was probably written between 1594 and 1596. *Greenblatt* in *The Norton Shakespeare* 805. With a characteristic improvement of the text before him, Shakespeare changed "Liar" to the friskier "lunatic." As for Southwell invoking God's authority for the writing of Spiritual

Sonnets, who can deny that Shakespeare had been given a hint and even a push?

The unmistakable interaction of the two poets, and its possible intensity, find a parallel in a modern pair. Arthur Miller and Elias Kazan – once friends united ideologically in a hostile Hollywood, then separated by their responses to harsh governmental pressure, each rebuking the other. *Miller* 333-334. In *The Crucible* Miller showed how a good man should resist his interrogators, Kazan in *The Waterfront* showing a good man beaten for his honesty. The analogy is not exact, merely suggestive.

Recently, John Klause has provided numerous examples of echoes of Southwell in Shakespeare. The multiplicity and the singularity of the echoes make it probable that they do not come from coincidence or some common source but are the result of Shakespeare's reading and retention of Southwell's writing. *Klause 2008*, 28-35. These echoes are as early as *Venus and Adonis. Id.* 47-51. They continue as late as *Measure for Measure,* in which the echoes are from Southwell's *Epistle of Comfort. Id.* 231-235. To give a single example, Southwell wrote,

> "Our infancy is but a dreame, our youth but a madnesse . . .
> our age a sicknesse."

The Duke, disguised as a friar, tells Claudio

> Thou hast nor youth nor age
> But as it were an after-dinner sleep
> Dreaming of both, for all thy blessed youth
> Becomes as aged and doth beg the alms
> Of palsied eld . . . .

Measure and Measure 3/1/34-35

Shakespeare has cherished Southwell's letter and transformed it. The "after-dinner sleep" is an unforgettable image. Elements of

Southwell remain and "palsied" echoes "palsy" used on the next page of Southwell's letter. The many instances identified by Klause of elements of the *Epistle of Comfort* (1587) now reassembled in *Measure for Measure* make the case that Shakespeare knew Southwell's work and drew on it years after it had been written and its author put to death. For over a decade the playwright looked for words, phrases, images, themes in Southwell's poetry and prose. He did not pillage nor plagiarize. He read the other's work knowledgeably, sensitively, selectively, transforming it into his own. Klause has demonstrated, first, Shakespeare's early knowledge of Southwell's compositions circulating only in manuscript within the Catholic community; second, Shakespeare's generous appreciation of Southwell's writing. It is this double demonstration that bolsters my belief that the poet who "brought a tomb" or tome was Southwell.

Southwell was not only older but theologically trained. It is not improbable that he took it on himself to hint that Shakespeare should do more. That Shakespeare responded, not slavishly but creatively, is not an unreasonable supposition. Southwell sought "a pheere" and found one in Shakespeare. If one pursues the clues, a pun can be found in "Dear eie" with which Southwell begins his poem to "the reader." "Eie" may not be mere metonymy but could stand for the addressee as "I" or as "my other self." As Shakespeare read Southwell's urgent prose, the alliterative "Spiritual Sonnets" could not help but meet his own eye.

The argument that Southwell is one of the Church's "two poets" may be reinforced by consideration of Sonnet 54, a sonnet not addressed to the Church, but possibly addressed to Southwell himself. I do not think the possibility constitutes proof of the addressee. At the same time, I think it would be a mistake to leave it unmentioned:

Sonnet 54
"O how much more doth beauty beauteous seem"

Oh how much more doth beauty beauteous seem,
By that sweet ornament which truth doth give,
The Rose looks fair, but fairer we it deem
For that sweet odour, which doth in it live:
The Canker blooms have full as deep a dye
As the perfumed tincture of the Roses.
Hang on such thorns, and play as wantonly
When summer's breath their masked buds discloses:
But, for their virtue only is their show,
They live unwoo'd, and unrespected fade;
Die to themselves. Sweet Roses do not so;
Of their sweet deaths, are sweetest odours made:
And so of you, beauteous and lovely youth,
When that shall vade, by verse distills your truth.

It's hard to read the first twelve lines of this sonnet except as allegory. They are not about horticulture. Who are meant by the roses marked by a canker, who have no odor, who die to themselves? Who are those who are ornamented by truth, who die yielding a sweet odor? Booth does not attempt to say. The kinds of rose are contrasted as were the flowers and the weeds. The allegory refers to groups not to a single individual. Beauty and truth act, as in *Loves Martyr*, as markers of the Church or her members.

"Hang" at the start of line 7 strikes an ominous note. The canker buds hang on. They also die. But they do not hang or die as martyrs. They die to themselves. In contrast, the roses marked by truth die "sweet deaths," of which the odors that are "sweetest" are made. Whose deaths have such odors?

The summer's flow'r is to the summer sweet

Though it itself it only live and die

So Sonnet 94 praises the virginal. In Sonnet 54, the flowers who die to themselves are unrespected, that is, paid no attention. *Booth* 226. Worse, they have cankers. The differing valuations of virginity may be accounted for by supposing the two sonnets stem from different occasions. A parallel case is the positive use of "fools of time" in Sonnet 124 and the negative use of the same phrase in Sonnet 116.

The valuation of virginity here is made to heighten a contrast with those whose deaths yield a sweet odor. They are those who rank highest among mortals. They must be the martyrs.

This deduction is confirmed by the sole addressee of Sonnet 54, a beauteous and lovely youth. Has not the poet abandoned allegory? Is he not speaking one-on-one to the one his verse shall celebrate? Unarguably, not a group but a person is now addressed. His death is one of the deaths of Roses whose odor is sweet. The question remains, How is this personal communication connected to the twelve lines that precede it?

A connection would exist if the addressee were a poet likely to be a martyr. I propose one martyr whom Shakespeare knew, to whom he could have spoken here: Robert Southwell, S.J. The addressee is incontestable; the lovely youth of line 13. He is one person. He has attributes exciting the affection and admiration of the poet. His poetry speaks truth.

Line 14: "that" must refer to youth as a quality. The sense is when you age, your poetry will convey your truths.

Many editors emend "by" to "my" in line 14. The emendation is not necessary. *Booth* 227 judiciously concludes that emendation is defensible, but he notes that "distills" is intransitive. Leaving the line unchanged, it is a tribute to the poetry of the person celebrated and a concluding acknowledgment of the truth the poetry conveys. But indisputably the addressee is younger than Shakespeare. If so, he cannot be Southwell, over two years the poet's senior. Q.E.D.

Such logic disallows license to the poet, who is moved by the anticipated death of his friend and who speaks of him as he remembers him before his capture: a youth. Such is my suggestion, not demonstration but an hypothesis too rash to defend with confidence and noted as no more than possible. I do not claim sonnet 53 as one of the Twenty-two.

Sonnet 143 appears in the sequence of sonnets usually seen addressed to a woman.

Sonnet 143.
"Lo, as a careful housewife runs to catch"

Lo, as a careful housewife runs to catch
One of her feather'd creatures broke away,
Sets down her babe, and makes all swift dispatch
In pursuit of the thing she would have stay.
Whilst her neglected child holds her in chase,
Cries to catch her whose busy care is bent

To follow that which flies before her face,
Not prizing her poor infant's discontent;
So runn'st thou after that which flies from thee,
Whilst I thy babe chase thee afar behind;
But if thou catch thy hope, turn back to me,
And play the mother's part, kiss me, be kind.
So will I pray that thou mayst have thy *Will*,
If thou turn back and my loud crying still.

For a reader of the Gospels, the opening lines of Sonnet 143 call to mind the words of Jesus to the city of Jerusalem:

How often would I have gathered thy children together as the henne gathereth her chickens under her wings

Matthew 23:37

The image of the motherly hen was set irremovably before Christians. Shakespeare adopts it, changing the image of Christ as the mother hen by substituting the body of Christ, the Church, and turning the hen into a housewife minding chickens.

The Church is pictured in pursuit of what flies from her, the restoration of her place in England. Embarked on what is seen by the housewife as an imperative, she neglects her baby. The use of this metaphor in Lines 7 and 8 recalls the use of "babe" in Sonnet 115 as a pun, one reading of which is a metaphor for the poet's immature love, capable of growth. Here "babe" is not capitalized. With an italicized pun on "will," line 13 identifies the neglected infant with the poet (thy will or thy Will).

The emphatic closing couplet also drops metaphor and simile and speaks openly in the poet's own voice: "I pray." This plea is not to be read as a conventional "please" but taken literally as expressing the poet's action. His prayer is that Mother Church will be motherly and that she will mercifully receive her loudly wailing child. The poem changes the penitent's posture. Asking for kindness, the poem makes a kind of complaint. The Church has not paid attention to him. Arguably, the Church's neglect of critical Catholics like the poet is implied.

The spectacle of A pursuing B who is in the same plight as she pursues C is as good comedy in Gilbert and Sullivan as it is in *As You Like It*:

Silvius:	[Love] is to be made of sighs and tears,
	And I am for Phoebe.
Phoebe:	And I for Ganymede.
Orlando:	And I for Rosalind
Rosalind:	And I for no woman.

As You Like It 5.3.75-78.

Something like this scenario seems to have influenced commentators who read the later sonnets as addressed to the poet's mistress. Sonnet 143 is a "preposterous little allegory," evidence of the poet's "reduction to infantile and irrational status." *Vendler* 601. A priori, this reading cannot be excluded even though Shakespeare is then viewed as a helpless, mindless creature and his actual creation in Sonnet 143 of a work of force and beauty is dismissed as "preposterous." Booth also finds the scene conjured up to be "ridiculous." He suggests that Shakespeare may have recalled two other instances of "chicken-related verse" in *The Canterbury Tales*. He contends that the situation portrayed "resembles" lines of Sonnet 142 "in which 'A' vigorously seeks 'B' while 'C' seeks 'A' with equal vigor." *Booth* 494.

A comic scenario can't be ruled out. But the scenario has problems. Booth acknowledges that "the manner and spirit of this sonnet are very different from what precede and follow" – a clue that something else is going on than the mocking of a mistress. The careful mother hen is a poor metaphor for a promiscuous slut. The chain of frustrated lovers does not form a round; it is broken by B not pursing C. Finally, could Shakespeare have been insensitive to the resonance of Matthew in the image he evoked?

The twelve poems addressed to the Church conclude with a sonnet that could be entitled "A Salute to the Church" and set as a climax to the dozen.

Sonnet 124.
"If my dear love were but the child of state"

If my dear love were but the child of state,
It might for fortune's bastard be unfather'd,
As subject to time's love or to time's hate,
Weeds among weeds, or flowers with flowers gather'd.
No, it was builded far from accident;
It suffers not in smiling pomp, nor falls
Under the blow of thralled discontent,
Whereto th' inviting time our fashion calls:
It fears not policy, that *Hereticke,*
Which works on leases of short-number'd hours,
But all alone stands hugely politic,
That it nor grows with heat, nor drowns with showers.
To this I witness call the fools of time,
Which die for goodness, who have lived for crime.

The Challenge. "The most extreme example of Shakespeare's constructive vagueness." *Booth* 419. "Its individual expressions have perplexed every reader." *Id.*, quoting T.G. Tucker. Does the vagueness and do the perplexities rest on a fundamental misreading?

Unlikely interpretation. The poem is conventionally classified as among the last of the poems on a man. The difficulty is the pronoun "it" used five times, forcefully interpreted to refer to the speaker's love for the addressee. *Booth* 423. But is one person's love "builded" (line 5)? Can it be witnessed in the way that lines 13 and 14 require? These two lines, *Booth* says at 423, are "vaguely phallic." But who is having sex?

Clues. The speaker's "dear love" is something apart from one that could be imagined as "the child of state" (line 1). It could live or die with its constituents (line 4). It is subject to pomp and to thralldom (line 6 and 7). These characteristics suggest not a person but an institution.

"fools of time" can mean "innocents." *The Taming of the Shrew* 3.2.153; *Booth* 424. Who are these innocents who are called as witnesses?

Q capitalizes and italicizes *Hereticke*.

Interpretation:

Lines 1-2. If the institution were only "the child of state," i.e., sponsored by the government, it would have lost its father. The supposition is contrary to fact.

Lines 3-4. If the supposition were true, the fortunes of the time would determine its existence and the fate of its constituent members. The lines incorporate imagery used in Sonnet 94. As in Matthew 7:26, the Church consists of the good wheat and the thistles or, as here expressed, of flowers and weeds, the images used in Sonnets 69 and 94 to describe the Jesuits. Each will have judgment at the end, and the end would be now if the Church could be ended by the state.

Line 5. "builded far from accident": "on this rock I will build my Church." Matthew 16:18, the Petrine pun on which the papacy is founded.

Line 6. "in smiling pomp" = the Church in the old regime. "thrallèd discontent" = the Church now. The Church survives the fortunes of the day.

Lines 9-10. The Church does not fear shortrun political decisions, often the way to heresy that at best gets a short lease. The capitalized "Hereticke" personifies doctrine that is rejected.

Line 11. "all alone stands hugely politic": the Church is wonderfully wise.

Line 12. "Nor grows with heat". The Church does not grow by rash action. A warning is implicit, as in the poems to the Jesuits. "nor drowns with show'rs". The Church survives the tempests = persecutions that menace.

Lines 13-14. "To this I witness call the fools of time": A triumphant pun: (1) To the truth of what I have stated about the Church I call as witness, and indeed as witness in the sense of martyr, the innocents indicated by line 14. (2) Myself an eyewitness to martyrdom, I testify.

Booth 424-425 writes of the final lines: ("An editor or student of the poem can easily respond to the couplet's sound of transparent simplicity by casting about for a specific group that Shakespeare might refer to: a century of reformation and counter-reformation provides any number of specific candidates [in England, Jesuit conspirators, Protestant martyrs under Mary, Roman Catholic martyrs under the other Tudors, etc.], but a choice is arbitrary"). The odd pair of double brackets are Booth's. The choice is arbitrary unless one sees that the rest of the poem celebrates the Church. The witnesses die for goodness, martyrs for the faith. In the eyes of the state they lived for crime. The martyrs Shakespeare had in mind are not to be brushed off by an etcetera or by claiming that a choice is arbitrary. The martyrs known to Shakespeare were Catholics. As line 14 states, he himself has been an eyewitness. To create a conflict, to press a paradox, he adopts the language of his adversaries.

Klause 1999, 229-230 observes that the entire sonnet has been "significantly influenced" by the *Humble Supplication* of Southwell. This work was composed in 1591. Southwell's capture prevented its publication, but it circulated in manuscript until its publication in 1600. See R. C. Bald, *Introduction to Southwell 1953* pp. xi-xiii. Southwell put in this way the case of the Catholics undergoing persecution for the sake of conscience:

But because we, like god Almightyes fooles (as some scornfully call us) lay our shoulders under every loade . . . . *Id*. 26.

The poet's perspective is Southwell's. Garnet wrote Aquaviva on May 2, 1597: "Catholics here are called God's fools, since, to their credit, they make themselves simpletons that they may become wise." *Caraman* 236. "God's fools" in Garnet is wholly positive. I quote the phrase not to show that Shakespeare was privy to Garnet's correspondence, but to suggest how the expression was current among the Catholics Shakespeare knew.

To sum up: the poet's dear love was not sponsored by the state nor built by chance; it has not met its end; it has known prosperity and adversity; it has not grown by rash impetuosity nor been destroyed by passing persecutions; it looks to the long run. The truth of what the poem proclaims is borne witness by the criminals who are killed for their faith and by Shakespeare himself. No stronger affirmation of the poet's love for the Church can be imagined.

10. Two To The Virgin Mother

The Catholic view of the Virgin saw her conceived without her inheriting the sin of Adam; as herself conceiving a child without sexual intercourse; and as thereby becoming the mother of a son who was also God. A modern secular mind is apt to see the first of these miracles as pointless, the second as mythological, and the third as unbelievable. Hence, the two Marian sonnets appear to be almost inaccessible to secular spirits. If they will enter in imagination into the world of Marian piety, they may see the point of the poetry.

Sonnet 109.
"O Never say that I was false of heart"

O Never say that I was false of heart,
Though absence seem'd my flame to qualify,
As easy might I from my self depart
As from my soul which in thy breast doth lie:
That is my home of love; if I have rang'd,
Like him that travels, I return again,

Just to the time, not with the time exchang'd,
So that myself bring water for my stain.
Never believe though in my nature reign'd,
All frailties that besiege all kinds of blood,
That it could so preposterously be stain'd,
To leave for nothing all thy sum of good:
For nothing this wide Universe I call,
Save thou, my Rose, in it thou art my all.

A lot, but not everything, depends on how the last two lines of this sonnet are read. Beyond dispute, the poet puts himself in the role of a lover who has failed the one he loves. The conventional reading ignores the religious resonances. Elucidation of this sonnet requires not only close reading but taking into account the immense devotional heritage which Shakespeare shared.

Lines 1-4. The poet has appeared to waver but his identity is fixed: his soul lies in the bosom of the addressee. As *Booth* 351 notes, lines 3-4 echo Ephesians, chapter 5. As already remarked, in that epistle the union of Christ and the Church becomes a pattern for the union of husband and wife. Shakespeare does not cite Scripture flatly but gives his citation a turn. Here his soul's close tie to the beloved is the most that is affirmed. In line 2, "flame" is chosen to express ardor. Like other references already noted in the Twenty-two, the flame is spiritual. In lines 3-4, "self" is distinct from "soul," but inseparable from it. In Line 4, the poet commits himself to a breast that is the host of his spiritual essence.

Lines 5-8. This breast is his "home of love." He returns to it like a traveler coming home. "Just to the time" is glossed by *Booth* 331 as "faithful to my appointed hour." The poet returns exactly at this hour or, alternatively, he rightly returns at this hour. Contrary to other sonnets' verses on the role of time, he has not changed ("exchanged") with time, that is, he is fundamentally what he's always been despite his departures. He has not changed but he is stained: so he weeps ("brings water.")

Booth 351 sees the speaker as acting with effrontery, "to display Falstaff-like gall in solemnly making a logical-sounding equation between two incomparable things, the journeys of a traveler and the promiscuous liaisons of an unfaithful lover." Insisting on a sexual interpretation of the metaphor, Booth transforms a plea to the Virgin into a "logical fraud," remarkable for its "grossness."

Shakespeare could provide a character with a sophistical rationalization of indefensible conduct, e.g., Prince Hal's soliloquy defending his association with low life:

> Yet herein I will imitate the sun
>
> Which doth permit the base contagious clouds
>
> To smother up his beauty from the world
>
> That when he please again to be himself
>
> Being wanted he may be more wondered at
>
> *Henry IV*, part I, 1.3.174-179.

The question is whether, in this sonnet, he indulges in such rationalization.

Booth acknowledges that "water" suggests tears of repentance, but finds "the solemnity of the line" undermined by the pun in line 9 ("reigned" or "rained"). I see not subversion but contrast: where once weakness reigned or rained, water now flows in regret.

Lines 9-12. Traveling has been an innocuous description of what are now suggested to have been a range of sins. Yet, so lines 11-12 make bold to suggest, it cannot be believed that his faults have been so unnaturally or perversely ("preposterously") committed as for him to leave for a random heap of nothing "all thy sum of good." Who is the one who contains this sum, the one to whom the poet speaks? The last line contains the answer. It is his "all." It is she who is addressed as "my Rose."

In Q, which I follow, "Rose" is capitalized. Again, the capitalization is not decisive but suggestive. According to *Booth* 354, "my rose" is a common way of expressing affection: "rose" is emblematic of perfections; it is understood as 'the best." Booth assumes that the best here is a special friend. Booth's assumption makes sense in terms of the conventional classification of the first batch of sonnets; if the echo of Ephesians is expunged, the language seeming to refer to sin is given a metaphorical meaning, and "rose" is reduced to the banal.

"Rose" is far from univocal in Shakespeare. Its meaning is controlled by context. If "my Rose" as used here is understood to be but a common form of endearment, the final two words of the poem function as flatly as "my honey" does in a 1940's musical. No! "My Rose" is at the apex of the word's meanings. It works to sum up the Marian piety, the trust in mercy through an intercessor, the love that binds the poet to the Virgin Mother. The rose is Mary.

Even before the popularization in the thirteenth century of the chain of prayers principally addressed to Mary and called the *rosarium* or rose garden, Mary had been associated with roses. A stream of poetry treated Mary herself as the rose, the best, the perfect person unstained by any sin, her own or her ancestors, and therefore immaculate. The fusion of the rose with Mary and the Church has been unforgettably memorialized by Henry Adams apropos of the western rose window of the cathedral of Chartres: "the Virgin designed this rose [and] placed it upon the breast of her Church – which symbolized herself." *Adams* 143. And Adams goes on to extol the unique importance of Mary in obtaining God's pardon for sinners. Chartres is tangible embodiment of the theme of Sonnet 109.

Take as an English example of the fifteenth century these verses of
"There is no rose of swych vertu":

> There is no rose of such virtue
>
> As is the rose that bore Jesus. Aleluia.
>
> For in this rose contained was
>
> Heaven and earth in little space.
>
> A wonder to be seen.

The rose, as the Mother of God, is celebrated by this poem as the
receptacle of the Trinity:

> By that rose we may well see
>
> That he is God in persons three.
>
> Made in equal form.

> *The New Oxford Book of Carols* 82-83; spelling modernized.

The metonymy is no secret. As another fifteenth century carol
puts it,

> A rose hath borne a lilly white

> *Greene*, n.174.

The rose is Mary, the lilly, Jesus. In the same tradition is the
Christmas carol celebrating the rose foretold by Isaiah that blooms in
the dark of winter and gives birth to a blossom who is Christ. Set to
music by Johann Sebastian Bach and still sung today, the words appear
in a collection of German carols as early as the sixteenth century. The
carol illustrates the antiquity, the longevity, and the attractiveness of
the identification of Mary with the flower. The rose easily stood for
Mary in the Catholic consciousness of Shakespeare's era.

Identifying the flower with the Virgin may seem a stretch to a
modern reader unlikely to cultivate an intense devotion to the Virgin
Mother. The simplicity, the boldness, even the extravagance suited
Shakespeare. These qualities that mark him also mark the Bible. The
poet who wrote an apotheosis of Anne Line could not have shrunk

from celebrating, albeit covertly, the greatest of the saints. His "sum of good," his best, is Mary.

That, in this context, the rose refers to Mary may be seen in the larger current of Marian devotion. Mary is not only the rose but she is the enclosed garden – the only human being (except her son) brought into existence without any stain of sin on her soul. Since the early thirteenth century struggle against the Cathars, a popular prayer of devotion to the Virgin, as well as an affirmation of the goodness of procreation, was the Ave Maria:

> Hail Mary, full of grace,
>
> The Lord is with you.
>
> Blessed are you among women
>
> And blessed is the fruit of your womb.

As early as the end of the eleventh century, the *Salve Regina*, going beyond the gospel presentation of Mary, had saluted her in these terms:

> *Salve Regina, Mater misericordiae,*
>
> *Vita, dulcedo, spes nostra, salve.*

In English: Hail, Queen, mother of mercy,

> Our life, our sweetness, and our hope, hail.
>
> *New Catholic Encyclopedia* 12, 2002

The literal-minded might have wondered how Mary could be "our life;" but the poem, celebrating Mary's unique role in salvation history, was not trammeled within the traces of the literal. In the sixteenth century, a Christian confident that Christ had offered himself as the sole sacrifice necessary for salvation might have balked at seeing Mary as "our hope." But such was the Catholic appreciation of her as intercessor with her son.

That Shakespeare elsewhere had this hymn in his mind is suggested by an unexpected riff on another phrase from it. The prayer to Mary speaks of us "weeping and wailing in this vale of tears." Southwell

entitled a lyric "A Vale of Teares." *St. Robert*, p. 36. Othello, referring
to his age, sees himself

> declined/Into this vale of years
>
> *Othello* 3.3.265-266.

This combination of words is a variation on Southwell or the
prayer. A glide from "vale of tears" accounts for the Moor's vale of
age.

The first line of the Hail Mary itself is echoed and expanded in
Cassio's salute to Desdemona as she lands on Cyprus:

> Hail to thee, lady, and the grace of heaven
>
> Before, behind thee, and on every hand
>
> Enwheel thee round!
>
> *Othello* 2.1.86-88.

At a minimum the greeting exhibits Shakespeare's knowledge of
this most familiar of Catholic prayers and his genius in varying the
familiar. More than that, in his invention of the verb "enwheel" – not
known to have been used before him – he has created a mobile metaphor
for grace: it surrounds and simultaneously enables its recipient to move
with more than her own power about an axis or center.

The salute to Desdemona enlarges, embroiders, and enriches
the Hail Mary. As for Cassio's speech by itself, you can reach one of
two conclusions: How easily Shakespeare adapts prayer to Mary to
a secular purpose! How familiar to him must have been the prayer!
Neither passage in *Othello* decides the meaning of Sonnet 109. They
do suggest how at home the poet was with homely Marian devotion.

Marian devotion had flourished in Britain under Queen Mary. In
1554, Edward Bonner, bishop of London, had written that God was
present more to Mary than to the angels; to be "true members of the
catholyke church" Christians should pray the Hail Mary often. Bishop
John White stressed Mary's special role as intercessor with unique

access to her son. Bishop Cuthbert Turnstall in his *Certain Godly and Devout Prayers* (1558) sought forgiveness of sins through the merits of Christ and the merciful intercession of Mary. *Wiziman in Swanson* 239-240.

Under Elizabeth, the horrified reaction of devout Protestants prevailed, typified in Foxe's *Acts and Monuments* by his characterization of the belief in Mary's intercessory role as blasphemy. *Freeman in Swanson* 229. Hazards existed in open praise of Mary. A courtier has

> ... whispered "By Jesu," so often that a
>
> Pursevant would have ravish'd him away
>
> For saying of our Ladies psalter.

John Donne, Satires IV.15-17.

The example is poetic exaggeration; the opprobrium attached to Marian devotion was a reality. Fierce rejection of the religion of the past did not obliterate the lessons learned from the older books and long embodied in the practices of people bred in the ways of their mothers.

Victory over the Turk at Lepanto was often ascribed to people praying the rosary, and in 1573, Gregory XIII had instituted the feast of Our Lady of the Most Holy Rosary. Before Garnet came to England, he, a Jesuit, took pains to secure from Sesto Fabri, the general of the Dominicans, authority to admit English Catholics into the Confraternity of the Holy Rosary. Garnet's first book, printed clandestinely in 1593, was entitled The *Societe of the Rosary*. English Catholics, Garnet reported, were eager to be enrolled. Mary was not only "the rainbow" after the storm. She was seen both as the compassionate mother and, as an antiphon in a Byrd mass put it, the virgin who could "alone" crush all heresies. *Caraman* 143-145, 163.

The Jesuits in England continued to cherish Mary and to emphasize her unique role as advocate for sinners. The several Byrd masses in

Mary's honor have already been noted. In Southwell's spiritual poetry, Mary is a major figure. Writing of the death of Mary, Southwell used a phrase not far from line 12 of Sonnet 109:

The world doth loose the summ of all her blisse. . . .

By maryes death mankind an orphan is.

"The death of our Ladie," *St Robert*, p.11.

Using "flower" as metonymy for both Mary and Christ, he wrote:

For flower he is and in flower he breeded

"Christ returns out of Egypt." *Id.* 10.

Celebrating the presentation of Jesus and the purification of Mary, the poet did not hesitate to use a commercial metaphor for a spiritual transaction:

If god were to be bought, not worldly pelfe

But thow wert fittest price next god himselfe

"The Presentation," *Id.* 9.

He made Mary his addressee:

O virgin breast, the heavens to thee incline,

In thee their joy and soveraigne they agnize . . .

Haile fairest heaven, that heaven and earth doth blisse,

Whose vertewes starres god summe of justice is.

"Our Ladies Salutation." *Id.* 5.

That Mary was the name of the Shakespeare's own mother is probably not irrelevant. For a connoisseur of paradox, what greater paradox than that of the Virgin Mother? In the development of Christian doctrine, the paradox, the mystery had been doubled. The offspring of this entirely human woman was divine. As the Council of Chalcedon had confirmed, Mary was the *theokotos*, the God-bearer. As the prayer of ordinary Catholics greeted her, she was the mother of God. These three words combined the mystery of the Incarnation of God in human flesh with acknowledgment of the human cooperation by which the divine intervention in humanity had been accomplished.

For the repentant sinner how strong was the sense that Mary was the channel of mercy! In Michelangelo's *Last Judgment* in the Sistine Chapel a figure clutches a rosary held by one of the redeemed on the right of Christ. The figure is possibly one of the lost. But as Leo Steinberg has pointed out in lectures, a diagonal line runs from the rosary to the arm of the man holding the rosary up to the Virgin. What is conveyed is not certainty for the clutcher but unextinguished hope. For a Catholic of Shakespear's generation, it would have been as unthinkable to be mute on Mary as to have been utterly silent on Mary, Queen of Scots. In Sonnet 109 the poet found his tongue, acknowledged his deficiency, and sought the Mother's aid.

"At home is Heaven" is a title of one of Southwell's poems, a title capturing Catholic eschatology. *St.* Robert, p. 48. A human being is a wayfarer, *homo viator*, as Christian prayer put it. The wayfarer is on the way to the *patria*, the homeland. So the *Salve Regina* offered the prayer to Mary, "Lead us home at last." In Sonnet 109 Mary herself becomes the poet's "home of love": she leads us to where she is. As in Southwell, she is the world's "sum" of good. The rose that bore Christ, she is the poet's "all."

A second Marian sonnet follows on the heels of Sonnet 109. To reiterate a vital point, proximity alone is insufficient to determine a sonnet's meaning. Sonnet 110, indeed, is arguably not to Mary but to the Church. On balance, the addressee is Mary:

Sonnet 110.
"Alas! 'tis true, I have gone here and there"

Alas! 'tis true, I have gone here and there,
And made my self a motley to the view,
Gor'd mine own thoughts, sold cheap what is most dear,
Made old offences of affections new;
Most true it is, that I have look'd on truth
Askance and strangely; But, by all above,
These blenches gave my heart another youth,
And worse essays prov'd thee my best of love.
Now all is done, have what shall have no end,
Mine appetite I never more will grind
On newer proof, to try an older friend,
A God in love, to whom I am confin'd.
Then give me welcome, next my heav'n the best,
Even to thy pure and most most loving breast.

"Alas tis true I have gone here and there" begins with an expression of sorrow for his sins (line 1), continues with a confession of them (lines 2-6), goes on to resolve not to sin again (lines 7-12) and ends with a prayer to be welcomed back (lines 13-14). The order of the poem follows the prescription for receiving the sacrament of penance — sorrow for the sins one has committed; an enumeration of what they were; and a declaration of a firm purpose of amendment. The climactic couplet dares to ask that the poet, now absolved, be received with love by a maternal breast.

Line 3 "Gor'd mine own thoughts": see Southwell apropos the Catholics compelled to conformity and so "to live with a goared Conscience." *Southwell, A Humble Supplication*, p.4. The unusual application of a sharp instrument to an inner intangible is Southwell's invention. Characteristic Shakespearean variations are the changes from "Conscience" to "thoughts" and from the passive "goared" to the active "gored."

The specific sins the poet confesses are theological. He has strayed from the fold ("gone here and there"), making a fool of himself ("a motley"). He has "looked on truth/Askance". As *Booth* 365 remarks, truth is "commonly used in religious contexts to indicate revealed truth," as in the First Letter of John 2:21; such, I believe, is the sense here. To be a "looker-on" was not admirable. To look on truth "Askance and strangely" was to be in a worse posture. The poet has done violence to his own mind ("gored") and in order to gain worldly advantage has abandoned his own beliefs ("sold cheap what is most dear"). He has by later loyalties ("affections new") repeated his "offenses old". He has learned from his errors – the bright side, unusual in a confession and confirmed with his closing declaration, a variation on the "happy fault" of Adam. His swervings ("blenches") gave him the chance to learn by trial and error. These experiments ("essays") "proved" (tested or demonstrated) what was his "best of love."

The poet pledges that he has reformed. He will not experiment again to test a friend older than the errors he embraced. He is now committed to the one God. In Q, "God" is capitalized; one need not rely on the capitalization but on what John teaches: "God is love" 1 John 4:9, while Ephesians 2:4 speaks of "God's great love wherewith he loved us." The poet, offering a variation, entrusts himself to "a

God in love." That the indefinite article "a" is used before "God" does
not suggest polytheism. Biblical usage sanctioned it – for example,
"the Lord your God is a jealous God." Deuteronomy 6:16. What is
Shakespearian is to speak of a God in love.

For a Christian to speak of his God as "a God" may still seem odd.
The same usage may be found in Southwell:

> For heavenly floure shee is the Jesse rodd
>
> The child of man, the parent of a god.
>
> > "Our ladies Nativitye," *St. Robert*, p. 4.

In Line 9, *Booth* 356 finds "strong suggestions of 'heaven', 'eternal
reward' and 'posthumous bliss'." Booth's reference, spelled out, is to
"world without end," the translation of *saecula saeculorum* in the Latin
mass signifying the eternity of God. Shakespeare has adapted this
phrase to state the lasting character of his commitment.

Affirming his adhesion to God, the poet asks for welcome from a
mother who is at the same time pure and "most most loving." As in
Southwell, it is her breast that he seeks. The pure or virginal breast
overflows with love. The poet's "best" of Sonnet 109 is now qualified
as his best next to God. At the same time, with a pun on "next," she is
put next to heaven. This addressee is not the Church, but Mary.

This ranking of Mary is matched in Southwell:

> If god were to be bought for worldly pelfe
>
> But thou were fittest price nex god himself.
>
> > "The Presentation," *St. Robert*, p. 9.

Sonnet 110 either ends with a spiritual paean or a proclamation
of sexual passion. The breast that is sought could, in Shakespeare,
be male or female. The conventional commentators, assuming that
the poem addresses a young male, implicitly and unblinkingly accept
the idolatry; in their view, a sacramental form is employed to express
regret for infidelity to the poet's friend. The idolatry climaxes in

placing the friend next to heaven. As *Booth* 358 expresses the matter, his construction of "next my heav'n the best" makes it "a piece of evidence for the literal truth of the hyperbolic metaphor it asserts: the construction actually confuses the beloved and heaven . . .. The epithet does not assert the speaker's idolatry but demonstrates it."

Consistently with this position, *Booth* 359 dismisses the obvious meaning of "most, most" as the equivalent of "very, very" and declares: "most most loving breast carries perverse overtones like those embodied in so many of the phrases that precede it: 'most most loving' suggests 'most most-loving,' 'most many-loving,' 'most promiscuous'" so that the male addressed is presented "as the champion practitioner" of sexual infidelity. The hyphen added to "most-loving" that sets off this chaim of remarkable speculation is Booth's. It is not in a standard modern edition nor in Q.

As Booth reads the poem, the beloved's accusation of infidelity on the poet's part is turned back upon the beloved, who is mocked as the most unfaithful of lovers. This reading requires the reader to accept an extraordinary combination of idolatry and irony packed into fourteen lines. Recognizing the poet's capacity for paradox, can one still find that the sonnet hangs together?

Does the poet "literally" identify a man with heaven? In almost the same breath, does he rebuke him as particularly promiscuous? Does a sonnet that begins with confession of error and proceeds to a plea for mercy really end in a surly *tu quoque*? The incoherence of such interpretation underlines the difficulty in treating a Marian hymn as a conflicted, even disillusioned, squeal to a human lover. It's a difficulty magnified by Booth's change of the poem's punctuation in order to sustain his argument.

The climatic couplet is not a disillusioned squeal. It is a prayer. It is spoken to the Virgin and Mother who overflows with love for a sinner who has come home.

11. *Two to God*

Sonnet 122.
"Thy gift, thy tables, are within my brain"

Thy gift, thy tables, are within my brain
Full character'd with lasting memory,
Which shall above that idle rank remain
Beyond all date even to eternity.
Or at the least, so long as brain and heart
Have faculty by nature to subsist,
Till each to raz'd oblivion yield his part
Of thee, thy record never can be miss'd.
That poor retention could not so much hold,
Nor need I tallies thy dear love to score.
Therefore to give them from me was I bold
To trust those tables that receive thee more,
To keep an adjunct to remember thee
Were to import forgetfulness in me.

Sonnet 125.
"Were't ought to me I bore the canopy"

Were't ought to me I bore the canopy,
With my extern the outward honouring,
Or laid great bases for eternity,
Which proves more short than waste or ruining?
Have I not seen dwellers on form and favour
Lose all and more by paying too much rent
For compound sweet; Forgoing simple savour,
Pitiful thrivers, in their gazing spent?
No, let me be obsequious in thy heart,
And take thou my oblation, poor but free,
Which is not mix'd with seconds, knows no art,
But mutual render, only me for thee.
Hence, thou suborned *Informer*, a true soul
When most impeach'd, stands least in thy control.

Sonnets 122 and 125, not set next to each other, are related to each other and to God and the gifts given by God. Booth discusses the bawdy sense of "tables" as female genitalis and observes, "This sonnet is full of material for sexual innuendo that is never developed." *Booth* 415. If never developed, how is it relevant?

The first two words of Sonnet 122 are "Thy gifts." The next two words, "thy tables," identify what theological tradition held to be given by God to every rational creature – the commandments of natural law.

"Tables" is used in the sense that it is employed in the collection of laws entitled, "The Twelve Tables," designating the prescriptions of early Roman law, or as "table" is used to refer to the Ten Commandments as "the table of the law." Elsewhere Shakespeare uses the word in this sense. For example, the Duke of Clarence attempting to dissuade the two men sent to murder him expostulates:

> Erroneous vassals, the great King
>
> Hath in the table of his law commanded
>
> That thou shall do no murder.
>
> *Richard III* 4.4.83-85.

Another instance: Lucio says,

Thou concluded like the sanctimonious pirate who went to sea with the Ten Commandments, but scraped one out of the table.

> *Measure for Measure* 1.2.9.

The pirate eliminated either the commandment against murder or the commandment against theft. In Sonnet 122, the tables are the prescriptions of the natural law. In theological writing these prescriptions were often said to be the same as the Ten Commandments. *St. Thomas*, I-II, q.199, art. 2. Revelation duplicated nature. Either by promulgation on Mount Sinai or by inscription in rational nature, the commandments are the gifts of God to humankind.

The first six lines of the poem declare the special status of these gifts. St. Paul had written:

For when the Gentiles, which have no Lawe, do of Nature thy ways contayned in the Lawe: then they havying no Lawe, are a Lawe unto them selves. Which shews the effect of the Lawe written in their hearts.

> Rom 2:14-15.

Shakespeare varies the synecdoche by which "heart" stands for the person and speaks of the law as "written within my brain." Line

2 indulges in a pun: the brain is written on ("charactered"), at the same time the writing gives the brain character. As line 5 suggests, "brain" and "heart" are alternative ways of saying that the natural law is ingrained. St. Paul's text in echoed by lines 6-7 identifying the duration of the law as lasting as long as nature exists – as long as brain and heart have "faculty by nature to subsist," until in death ("razed oblivion") the law ends with the end of life.

This identity of the law with one's nature is emphasized by contrasting the imprint of the natural law with mere memory. Nature's imprint is superior to "that idle rank." As line 8, addressing God, drives home, "thy record," that is, the imprint of natural law, cannot be unknown ("missed"). It doesn't depend on memory, which is fallible ("poor retention"). The poet doesn't need notches ("tallies"), used to record a debt, in order for him to know his debt to God. The poet has given away as unneeded what would function like tallies, i.e., written copies of the commandments of natural law. The concluding couplet is emphatic: such "an adjunct" to what God has given would imply – a reductio ad absurdum – that he could forget what constitutes his nature.

Hamlet declares to his father's ghost that he will seek justice for his father's murder in terms that are analogous:

> Yea, from the table of my memory
> I'll wipe away all trivial fond records
> All saws of books, all forms, all pressures past
> That youth and observation copied there
> And thy commandment all abone shall live
> Within the book and volume of my brain,
> Unmix'd with baser matter

Hamlet 1.5. 98-104.

The ghost's command is so paramount that it functions as the single commandment inscribed in the tablet or table of the son's brain.

The thought of Sonnet 125 "Were't ought to me that I bore the canopy" is too complex to be a hymn to God in the Eucharist, but in the small compass of fourteen lines it is a celebration of the Eucharist. It begins with an invocation of the feast upon which the bread, now consecrated as the body of Christ, was carried in procession. It ends with a defiance of the priest-hunter who would intrude upon the mass. It reaches its climax in the third quatrain.

The great occasion on which the canopy was employed was Corpus Christi. Then the Eucharist was carried in a solemn procession beneath the canopy. The bearers of the canopy, at least at some times and places, were laymen. As canopy-bearers, they were incorporated into the liturgy. *Rubin* 247-248. These bearers were usually prominent persons but sometimes were boys. *Id*. 251.

"Then came the body of Christ under the canopy," wrote Marin Sanudo, observing a Corpus Christi procession in Venice in 1593. *Sanudo* 369. The connection of "the canopy" to the Eucharist is taken for granted by the diarist on the continent as it would have been by a Catholic in England.

Corpus Christi was a devotion specifically promoted by the Jesuits on mission to England. They focused on the feast of "that Divine Sacrament, which our Heretickes have sought so much to dishonor." *Brett* 154, quoting Robert Persons, S.J. Henry Garnet records in 1605 how he observed "Corpus Christi day with great solemnity and music and the day of the octave made a solemn procession about a great garden." *Caraman* 320. Byrd gave particular prominence to his own work for the feast. *Brett* 153. To have ignored Corpus Christi in writing the sonnets would have been as surprising as if Shakespeare had ignored Mary. The centrality of the feast in the Catholic understanding of the Eucharist made it peculiarly appropriate for him to commemorate.

Article XXVIII of *The Thirty-Nine Articles* explicitly denied the Catholic doctrine of transubstantiation as "repugnant to the plain words of Scripture" and went on in a paragraph beginning "Corpus Christi" to say, "The Body of Christ is given, taken, and eaten in the Supper only after an heavenly and spiritual manner." Further, "the Sacrament of the Eucharist was not by Christ's ordinance reserved, carried about, lifted up, or worshipped." *The Thirty-Nine Articles* 382. Only a Catholic would think of carrying the canopy.

The opening line asks if it makes any difference to the poet that he has carried the canopy. The second word "ought" may be read as "anything" or as "nothing." The natural implication of the line is that Shakespeare has himself been a canopy bearer. Corpus Christi processions were banned as of 1548. No indication exists that Stratford disobeyed the ban. But the neighboring town of Coventry held Corpus Christi processions as late as the 1570's, *Duffy* 582, 587, and if the Lancaster hypothesis is correct, Shakespeare would have had a chance to carry a canopy while staying with the Hoghtons. We need, however, not think that the poet speaks literally. The line may simply be meant to evoke his Catholic upbringing. With his body ("extern") he has honored the bread that is "the outward" of the Eucharist.

The first quatrain goes on to enlarge upon the Catholic education he received. He learned the foundations of the faith ("great bases for eternity"). "Which" in line 4 takes all of line 3 as its antecedent. The laying of the foundations has not survived "waste or ruining." Hence his question, What's it to him that he once upon a time was devout and docile in being catechized?

The second quatrain sets out to answer this question indirectly and abruptly by stating what has happened to contemporaries who have traded away their faith. They have dwelt in formalities and in the favor of the establishment. Making compromises ("compound sweet"), they have paid too much. The metaphor is mixed, combining the image of tenants for a time with the image of eaters of a delicacy. They have lost "all" that they hoped to preserve and they have lost "more" than all that. What they have lost is "simple savor" or, to read the pun, the Saver or Saviour.

The compromisers are contemptible or pitiable as "pitiful" may alternatively be read. Such is their state although in the world they thrive. Disgusted by this spectacle, the poet prays to be once again one of the faithful, dutiful ("obsequious") as he rests in Christ's heart. He offers himself as a sacrifice to God ("oblation"). It is an unworthy ("poor") sacrifice but one freely made. It is the real thing ("not mixed with seconds"). He gives himself to God in order to receive God ("only me for thee."). As Southwell had put it:

Gods gift am I, and none but God shall have me.

"The Nativity of Christ," *St. Robert* 7.

In the prayers at mass preceding the consecration of the bread and wine, *oblatio* is twice used:

This oblation (*oblatio*), therefore, of our service and of your whole family, we ask you, Lord, to accept graciously so that you dispose our days in your peace so that we are delivered from eternal damnation and numbered in the flock of your elect. Through Christ our Lord. Amen. . . .

This oblation (*oblatio*), do you, God, deign to make in all things blessed, approved, ratified, reasonable and acceptable, so that it may for us become the body and the blood of your most loved Son, our Lord, Jesus Christ.

After the consecration, the offering is described as "a pure victim (*hostia*), a holy victim, a stainless victim." Shakespeare moves "pure" from *hostia* to *oblatio* and plays with the difference: the offering of himself is not pure, it is poor, but it is free.

The concluding couplet rings with the same horror of the Informer that infuses energy into the *Loves Martyr* poem. The term is not only capitalized by Q but italicized. The Informer is, of course, imagined as bribed ("suborned") After he is driven away, the poet keeps his own courage up, reminding himself of the constancy of the martyrs.

Booth comes close to tracking the true meaning but nowhere does he swing more wildly from it. In one long paragraph at the end of his analysis, he enumerates elements in the poem that evoke the Holy Communion service as set out in the *Book of Common Prayer*. The "desired effect" of Holy Communion is that we "evermore dwell in Christ and he in us." The prayer before the consecration of the host is to God the Father, who gave his son to suffer on the cross where the son "by his one oblation" made satisfaction for the sins of the world. After communion is received, the communicants pray: "And here we offer and present unto Thee, O Lord, our selves, our souls and bodies to be a . . . . Sacrifice unto thee . . . ." Booth goes on to note that the instructions for buying the bread for communion specify "the best and purest wheat bread" with the implication that "the seconds" in commercial flour were not to be purchased. Booth further observes that those not receiving communion are castigated as "lookers on them that do Communicate." He concludes: "All in all, there is a great deal of inviting evidence for seeing this sonnet in relation to Holy Communion." *Booth* 429-430.

The relation that Booth contemplates is that of analogy, the analogy between the devout celebration of Holy Communion and the poet's love of a young man. He continues: "the analogy is never applied or activated while the poem is in process." In short, the sonnet's references to the communion service are for him an ineffective effort to compare the poet's love of a man to a believer's offering of himself to

God. What in truth is an extraordinary expression of love for God is reduced by this critic to a set of references that do not work.

Booth has made his task more difficult by supposing that the references must be to the service in the Church of England, not to the Catholic mass, which, in general, the service tracks. He mentions the custom of the canopy covering the host without noting that Corpus Christi processions were now illegal. He is at a loss to explain the suborned informer of Line 13. No Holy Communion service in the Church of England was in danger of such a creature, so how does his appearance fit into the supposed analogy? It does not. Booth is driven to imagining the informer as "a self-serving toady," who has accused the poet of infidelity to his beloved. But on reflection on the "thou," "thee," and "thy" which the poem employs, Booth reaches the "disconcerting" conclusion that the informer is the beloved addressee himself! *Id.* 429. The capitalized and italicized Informer boggles Booth. Neither of his alternatives makes sense. The toady is Booth's invention. A sudden charge against the person to whom the poet has just offered himself as an oblation is incredible.

Booth's commentary is completed by comparing the failed analogy of Holy Communion to "a thin thread of potentially bawdy references in the poem" – among them "frivolous references to premature ejaculation." *Id.* 430. These references like those Booth sees to the Eucharist are found by him to be inactivated and not integrated into the poem as a whole. Unactivated metaphors are like unactivated bombs. They are detritus unless exploded by the unwary or the officious. A poem comprehensible as a work of devotion to God, employing the language of the liturgy, becomes in the critic's reading a jumble of a failed analogy, inactivated images of sex, and the inexplicable characterization of the beloved as the bribed informer.

A distinctly different view of Sonnet 125 may be gained from this passage in *The Imitation of Christ*:

Non est enim oblatio dignior et satisfactio major pro peccatis quam se ipsum pure et integre cum oblatione corporis Christi in missa et in communione Deo offerre.

In English:

For there is no oblation more worthy nor satisfaction greater for sins

Than purely and entirely to offer your very self to God together with the oblation of the body of Christ in the mass and in communion.

De imitatione Christi: 4, ch. VII.

The thought is theological: In the mass, Christ is the perfect oblation; the believer may join himself as an oblation – in the poet's words, "poor but free."

The offering of oneself is connected in the mass to the boldest of prayers. Offering the simple bread and wine prior to the consecration, the celebrant mingles drops of water with the wine and prays:

Deus, qui humanae substantiae mirabiliter condidisti et mirabilior reformasti, da nobis per huius aquae et vini mysterium eius divinitatis esse consortes, qui humanitatis nostrae fieri dignitatus est particeps, Jesus Christus, Filius tuus, Dominus noster.

In English:

God, who wonderfully created the dignity of human substance and who has more wonderfully restored it, grant that by the mystery of this water and wine we may become co-sharers of the divinity of him who deigned to become a participant in our humanity, Jesus Christ, your Son, our Lord.

The poet whose beliefs in fact emerges from Sonnet 125 is the man who speaks in all of the Twenty-two. He is a sinner immersed in the spirit of the Gospel. He uses and varies biblical images and liturgical language with easy familiarity and freshness. He has taken to heart the most penetrating pages of St. Paul. The passion he brought to his sins he brings to his penitence. The Church will forgive him; Mary will intercede for him; Christ in the Eucharist receive him.

12. Recapitulation and Conclusion

As the Irish poet has put it,

Shakespearean fish swam the sea, far away from land.

Yeats 240.

I have not trolled for all these distant creatures, only for those in the *Loves Martyr* poem and certain of the Sonnets. I believe that I have landed these, that is, identified them, inspected them, brought to light their assumptions, background, and context, assayed their sense, and shown their spiritual significance.

I have begun this task with the sketch of a community created against its will by the statutes commanding religious conformity. Spectacularly, if sporadically, enforced, these statutes shape a common consciousness, in which martyrs hold a high place. Among the members of the community William Byrd may be found composing a motet or a mass; Robert Southwell can be glimpsed versifying in honor of the Virgin; Henry Garnet is heard reporting to Rome on the band of criminal missionaries he leads; and "Mrs. Martha" may be seen busy with the boardinghouse she runs for the itinerant criminals.

William Shakespeare has come to town and encountered this community. On the Arden side of his family his Catholic connections are clear. He has two Catholic schoolmasters and a schoolmate who became a Jesuit. He himself is seen by a disgruntled rival as "a crow," an epithet employed with religious venom. The young writer knows Southwell's work enough to adopt lines from him and use them in plays as early as *A Midsummer Night's Dream*. In the same play he salutes Mary, the executed Queen of Scots. In *Twelfth Night* he pauses, for no dramatic reason, to recall "the old hermit of Prague," the executed Jesuit, Edmund Campion. In *Hamlet* he assumes the existence of Purgatory and models the final salutation to Hamlet himself on the Catholic burial hymn, "*In paradisum deducant te Angeli.*" In *Measure for Measure* he continues to draw on Southwell and takes his title and theme from the words of Jesus reported by Matthew on the rigorous reciprocity ruling the life of the spirit. It is this playwright, deep in the currents of the oppressed community, who knows Byrd by his connections at court; who has been instructed in the extraordinary ecclesiastical powers possessed by Garnet; who is touched by the hanging of Mrs. Martha and celebrates the martyr as a co-supreme of love. It is this professional writer who, among the many sonnets he composes and circulates – some commissioned, some gratuitous – has written those with spiritual themes and thrust.

The Twenty-two are scattered among the one hundred and fifty-four assembled into a book produced by a coalition of publishers and booksellers with little, if any, input by the author. Any assumption as to the unity of themes and subjects of the book is an obstacle to understanding the Twenty-two.

Conventional critics have to concede that, of the 154, the first 17 do not express the love of the poet for the man addressed; that the two sonnets to the poet's soul are not valentines; and that the sonnet celebrating Ann Hathaway holds no hint of adulterous love. Hence, at the start of any critical look at the sonnets, the critic knows that 20 do not belong to the convenient conventional category. If 20 do not fit this category, may not others also be patient of a sense other than the conventional?

Reclaiming the Twenty-two, I bring to bear two lights not regularly used to illuminate them – the beliefs and associations of the author as shown by the *Loves Martyr* poem and by his connection with Robert Southwell. I add an analogy: William Byrd. I emphasize the experience and posture of the Jesuit missionaries. I turn to texts of St. Paul, to the language of liturgy and books of deep devotion and to the words of the mass itself in order to identify those who are spoken to by the sonnets and to elucidate the poems' meaning. An extemporizer may put a sonnet to use for any occasion. The author's meaning is not to be found by guess, mystification, or disregard of historical context.

In part, my argument is negative. The unlikelihood of the conventional readings demonstrate their frailty. The demonstration clears the way for positive proof of their meaning. I proceed not to demonstration of a logical sort but by a way familiar to argument in astrophysics, ethics, and law. It is the way of persuasive coherence. The story sticks together and makes sense. Interlocking with each other, the Twenty-two confirm the interpretation offered of each.

Sexual passion or spiritual aspiration? When religious language can be employed to express sexual desire, it is difficult to discern the intended meaning. Choice seems arbitrary. Not so, when the sexual currents are admittedly subterranean and undeveloped as we have seen them acknowledged to be in Sonnet 125 ("potentially bawdy" references to premature ejaculation); in Sonnet 116 (an "undercurrent of frivolous sexual suggestion"); or in Sonnet 31 ("unexploited" sexual puns). Not so, when as in Sonnet 115, the energy of the sonnet is said to depend on "a sustained quibble" on a word absent from the sonnet. Not so, when Sonnet 94 undergoes endless interpretation because its actual subject, the Jesuit mission in England, is unrecognized. Not so, when Sonnet 116 is declared to be "an unfinished poem or one that Shakespeare abandoned in frustration," a poem whose eighth line then "does not deliver meaning" and whose last line is written off as "more grossly faulty" because it is said to be unrelated to the thirteen lines that precede it. Is it the poet who has failed to exploit his sexual suggestions and deliver meaning or do the failures lie with the conventional critics?

By way of contrast these six poems appear almost irresistibly spiritual once their central points are perceived:

Sonnet 66, "Tir'd with all these for restful death I cry" enumerates evils without relation to any love affair; it punningly deplores the disgrace of right or rite perfection (the mass itself). It complains of the censorship ("authority") that makes art tongue-tied. It laments the theological "folly" in control. It is a love poem to the lonely Church the poet will not leave.

Sonnet 94, "They that have pow'r to hurt and will do none" celebrates a group who "husband nature's riches from expense" – that is, they are vowed to celibacy. They are praised and they are warned. They can only be the Jesuit missionaries to England.

Sonnet 112, "Your love and pity doth the impression fill" addresses one who can overgreen the poet's bad; who is his "All the world"; who instructs him in what is right and what is wrong. Who else can this figure be but the Church? Confirmation comes in the last line: everyone but the poet thinks that the addressee is dead.

In Sonnet 73, "The time of year thou mayst in me behold," the Church herself is given a voice. It is not the poet (still well under fifty) who speaks of his shaking yellow leaves and ruined choirs. It is the Church, asleep, almost extinguished, who glows with the fire of the martyrs, nourished by what consumes her.

In Sonnet 124, "If my dear love were but the child of state," the poet summons the martyrs, "who die for goodness," as witnesses to the life of the Church, no child of state, not built by accident, surviving pomp and persecution, above time's love and time's hate.

In Sonnet 125, the first two lines recall the carrying of the covering of the Eucharist. The last two lines shake off the traitorous spy. Both beginning and ending are impenetrable by the conventional approach. At the heart of the poem the poet offers himself to God in the mass.

A critical Catholicism characterizes the Twenty-two. It is not a political creed: Shakespeare does not work to change the regime. He is not polemical seeking to refute the reformers' doctrines. He is not indulging a nostalgia manifesting merely a yearning for yesteryear. He is not sighing over a picturesque ruin, nor is he recalling any golden age. He utters living and life-sustaining words telling the Church his sorrow for his sins, asking the Church for pardon, expressing his love for the institution on earth and for its members beyond earth. He salutes Mary, his rose. He celebrates God, the author of the natural law, and God in the Eucharist at the unaltered altar.

If this interpretation of the Twenty-two is accepted, the poems depend on what they take to be realities – sin and grace-giving sacraments, prayer and God's answer to prayer. They incorporate belief in responsibility for one's acts and thoughts and one's deviation from the truth, a belief that man has the capacity to offend God and the capacity to speak to God, and a belief in the unearned, inexplicable gifts of God. The poems proclaim a tempered admiration of missionaries and an unrestrained appreciation of martyrs. They are declarations of love of the dying but not extinct Church, incandescent in her ashes; of the Virgin Mary, Mother of God; of God in the law he has written and at the communion table he inhabits.

Did Shakespeare the man share this vision of reality, these beliefs and these loves? We cannot know his soul. We can say what makes these works of a supreme sonneteer work. The poet, so Sonnet 124 punningly proclaims, is himself an eyewitness to the martyrdom of those who have lived for goodness. The poems are acts of his conscience.

The Twenty-two – the Spiritual Sonnets – explore, express, and celebrate the paradoxes that are the mysteries of faith: the soul thrives at the expense of the body's decay; the Church lives in the deaths of her members; the chastest lives are the most fruitful; the most most pure virgin is the most most merciful mother; the love between God and man can be constant and yet grow; material symbols can be spiritual realities; in a piece of bread and a cup of wine God gives himself to the believer.

In the religious tempests of the time, in the twilight of his beloved, in the middle of the ruined remains of her beauty, in the muddle of his own life, in his own return to the ruined foundations of his faith, Shakespeare gives himself to God, "oblation poor, but free."

References

A and others v. Secretary of State for the Home Department, 2005 UKHL 511.

AAS = *Acta apostolicae sedis* (Vatican City, 1909 –).

Adams, Henry, *Mont-Saint Michel and Chartres* (Boston: Houghton Mifflin Co., 1904).

Allen, William, *A Defense and Declaration Of The Catholike Churches Doctrine touching Purgatory, and prayers for the soules departed*, (Antwep, 1567), reprinted in English Recusant Literature 1558-1640, vol. 18.

Aquinas, Thomas, St., *Summa theologiae*, ed. Pietro Caramello (Turin: Marietti, 1952).

Arnold, Matthew, "Shakespeare" in Arnold, *Poetical Works*, ed. G. B. Tinker and H. E. Lowry (London: Oxford Univ. Press, 1989).
Asquith, Clare, *Shadowplay: The Hidden Beliefs and Coded Politics of William Shakespeare* (New York: Public Affairs, 2005).

Augustine, St., *De moribus ecclesiae catholicae et moribus Manichaeorum, Corpus Scriptorum ecclesiasticorum latinorum*, vol. 41.

Auchincloss, Louis, *The Collected Stories of Louis Auchincloss* (Boston: Houghton Mifflin Company, 1994).

Barton, Anne, "The One and Only," *The New York Review*, May 11, 2006, pp. 22-25.

Bate, Jonathan, *Soul Of The Age. A Biography Of The Mind Of William Shakespeare* (New York: Random House, 2009).

Bate, Walter Jackson, *Samuel Johnson* (New York: Harcourt, Brace, Jovanovich, 1975).

Bearman, Robert, "John Shakespeare's 'Spiritual Testament': A Reappraisal," *Shakespeare Survey* 56, 184 (Cambridge: Cambridge Univ. Press, 2003).

Beauregard, David N., *Catholic Theology in Shakespeare's Plays* (Newark: University of Delaware Press, 2008).

Bene, Charles, "Le *De Puritate Tabernaculi:* Testmaent spirituel d'Erasme?," *Actes du colloque international Érasme* (Geneva: Librairie Droz, 1990).

Benedictines of the Solemnes Congregation, ed., *Mass And Vespers With Gregorian Chant* (New York: Desclée and Co., 1957).

Bertaud, Émil, "Dialogues spirituelles," *Dictionnaire de Spiritualité* (Paris: Beauchesne, 1967), vol. 3, col. 841.

Bible, the. Biblical quotations are from a facsimile reprint of the translation of the New Testament made in Geneva and published in 1557, reprinted London: Samuel Hagster and Sons. The Geneva Bible was the English Bible most frequently quoted by Shakespeare, although he has been shown to have quoted several other English translations.

Booth, Stephen, *Shakespeare's Sonnets*. Edited with analytic commentary. (New Haven: Yale University Press, 1978).

Bossy, John, "The English Catholic Community 1603-1605" in *The Reign of James VI and I*, ed. Alan G. R. Smith (New York: St. Martin's Press, 1973).

Bray, Gerald, ed. *The Anglican Canons* 1529-1947 (Rochester, N.Y.: The Boydell Press, 1998).

Brett, Philip, *William Byrd and His Contemporaries. Essays and a Monograph*, ed. Joseph Kerman and Davitt Moroney (Berkeley: Univ. of California Press, 2006).

Brouillard, R., "Sanchez, Thomas," *Dictionnaire de théologie catholique*, vol. XIVa., col. 1071.

Brownlow, Frank, "Richard Topcliffe: Elizabeth's enforcer and the representation of power in King Lear", in *Dutton, infra*,161-178.

Caraman, Philip, S.J., *Henry Garnet 1555-1606 and the Gunpowder Plot* (New York: Farrar, Straus & Co., 1964).

"Martyrs of England and Wales," *New Catholic Encyclopeida II* (New York: McGraw Hill, 1967).

Cary, John, *John Donne* (Oxford: Oxford Univ. Press, 1994).

Chambrun, Clara Longworth, Countess de, *Shakespeare Rediscovered* (New York: Charles Scribner's Sons, 1938).

    Essential Documents never yet presented in the Shakespeare Case (Bordeaux: Delmas, 1934).

Cohen, Walter, "Various Poems," *The Norton Shakespeare*, ed. Stephen Greenblatt (New York: W. W. Norton & Company, 1997).

Daube, David. "Schlegel and Shakespeare," *Rechtshistorisches Journal* 3 (1984), 183-186; also *Collected Works of David Daube*, volume 4, *Ethics and Other Writings* (Berkeley, 2008), 347-349.

Devlin, Christopher, *The Life of Robert Southwell. Poet and Martyr* (New York: Greenwood Press, 1969).

    Hamlet's Divinity (London: Rupert Hart-Davis, 1963).

Dickson, Peter W., "Bardgate: Was Shakespeare a Secret Catholic? *Oxfordian. The Annual Journal of the Shakespeare Oxford Society* 6:109-127 (Fall 2003).

Dies irae, in F. J. E. Raby, *A History of Christian-Latin Poetry From The Beginnings To The Close Of The Middle Ages* (Oxford: at the Clarendon Press, 1953).

Donaldson, Ian, ed., *Ben Jonson* (Oxford: Oxford Univ. Press, 1985).

Donne, John, *The Complete English Poems*, ed. A. J. Smith (London: Penguin, 1971).

The Holy Sonnets, Variorum Edition of the Poetry of John Donne, ed. Gary A. Stringer, Vo. 7, part 1, (Bloomington, Ind.: Indiana Univ. Press, 2005).

Dronke, Peter, "The Phoenix and the Turtle", *Orbis Litterarum* Vol. 23, Issue 3, 199-220 (1968).

Duffy, Eamon, "Bare ruined choirs: remembering Catholicism in Shakespeare's England" in *Dutton, infra*, 40-57.

The Stripping Of The Altars. Traditional Religion In England 1400-1580 (New Haven: Yale Univ. Press, 1992).

Duncan-Jones, Kathcrinc and Woodhuysen, H.R., ed., *Shakespeare's Poems* (London, 2007: The Arden Shakespeare).

Dutton, Richard; Findlay, Allison; and Wilson, Richard, *Theatre and religion. Lancastrian Shakespeare* (Manchester and New York: Univ. of Manchester Press, 2003).

Dyce, Alexander, *The Poems of Shakespeare* (London: William Pickering, 1842).

Edmondson, Paul and Wells, Stanley, *Shakespeare's Sonnets* (Oxford: Oxford University Press, 2004).

Eliot, T. S., *Selected Essays, 1917-1932* (New York: Harcourt, Brace and Company, 1932).

Eliz. = *Statutes of the Realm Published by Command of his Majesty King George The Third* (Buffalo, N.Y.: Hain and Co., 1993).

Emerson, Ralph Waldo, *Parnassus* (1874), reprinted by Books For Libraries Press, Freeport, New York.

Finnis, John and Martin, Patrick, "Another Turn for the Turtle. Shakespeare's Intercession for Love's Martyr," *Times Literary Supplement*, April 18, 2003.

Flynn, Dennis, "Out of Step: Six Supplementary Notes on Jasper Heywood," *McCoog 2007, infra*, 233-275.

Gerard, John, *The Autobiography of a Hunted Priest*, translated from a Latin memoir by Gerard and edited by P.C. (= Philip Caraman) (New York: Pellegrino & Cudahy, 1952).

Girard, René, *A Theater of Envy. William Shakespeare* (New York: Oxford University Press, 1991).

Giroux, Robert, *The Book Known As Q. A Consideration of Shakespeare's Sonnets* (New York, Atheneum, 1982).

Graeka, Gregory, O.F.M., conv., "Christian Viaticum: A Study Of Its Cultural Background," *Traditio* 9, 1 (1953).

Gratian, *Concordia discordantium canonun, Corpus iuris canonici*, ed. E. Friedberg (Graz, 1959 reprint).

Greenblatt, Stephen, *Hamlet in Purgatory* (Princeton: Princeton Univ. Press, 2001)(herein cited as Greenblatt, Purgatory).

Will in the World. How Shakespeare Became Shakespeare (New York: W.W. Norton & Co., 2004).

Greene, Graham, "Introduction" to John Gerard, *The Autobiography of a Hunted Priest, Gerard, supra.*

The Virtue of Disloyalty (London: Bodley Head, 1972).

Greene, Richard Leighton, ed., *The Early English Carol* (Oxford: at the Clarendon Press, 1977).

Greer, Germaine, *Shakespeare's Wife* (London: Bloomsbury, 2007).

Gregory, Brad S., *Salvation at Stake. Christian Martyrdom in Early Modern Europe* (Cambridge: Harvard Univ. Press, 1999).

Grierson, Herbert, ed., *Donne's Poetical Works* (Oxford: Oxford Univ. Press, 1923).

Groves, Beatrice, *Texts and Traditions. Religion in Shakespeare 1592-1601* (Oxford: Clarendon Press, 2007).

Haigh, Christopher, *English Reformations. Religion, Politics and Society under the Tudors* (Oxford: Clarendon Press, 1993).

Hammerschmidt-Hummel, Hildegard, *The Life and Times of William Shakespeare* (London: The Chauser Press, 2007).

Hanley, Hugh, "Shakespeare's Family in Stratford Records," *Times Literary Supplement*, May 21, 1964.

Heal, Felicity. *Reformation in Britain and Ireland* (Oxford: Oxford Univ. Press, 2003).

Herbert, Mary Sidney: *The Collected Works*, ed. Margaret Hannap, Noel J. Kinnamon, and Michael G. Brennan (Oxford: Clarendon Press, 1998).

Herford, C. H. and Simpson, Percy, *Ben Jonson* (Oxford: at the Clarendon Press, 1954).

Heywood, Jasper, S.J., "The Lookers-on," *An Anthology of Catholic Poets*, ed. Shane Leslie (Westminster, Md.: The Newman Press, 1953).

Hogge, Alice, *God's Secret Agents. Queen Elizabeth's Forbidden Priests and the Hatching of the Gunpowder Plot* (New York: Harper Collins, 2005).

Holmes, Peter, *Resistance and Compromise. The Political Thought of the Elizabethan Catholics* (Cambridge: Cambridge Univ. Press, 1989).

Hutton, Charles A., "The Christian Basis of Shakespeare's Sonnet 146," *Shakespeare Quarterly*, vol. 19, p. 355 (Autumn, 1968).

Jackson, Ken and Marotti, Anthony, ed., *Shakespeare and Religion* (South Bend: Univ. of Notre Dame Press, 2011).

Jas. See Eliz.

Jones-Davies, Margaret, "Cymbeline and the sleep of faith" in *Dutton, supra*, 197-227.

Kelly, Christine J., "Anne Line," *Dictionary of National Biography* (2004).

Kerman, Joseph, *The Masses and Motets of William Byrd* (Berkeley: Univ. of California Press, 1981).
    "William Byrd" in *The New Grove Dictionary of Music and Musicians*, ed. Stanley Sudee (2d ed. 2001).
    "Byrd, William," Grove Music Online (accessed 7/21/06), http://www.grovemusic.com/shared/views/article. html?seciton=music.04487.4>.

Kerrigan, John, ed., *William Shakespeare. The Sonnets and A Lover's Complaint* (New York: Viking, 1986).
    Archipelagic English Literature, History and Politics 1603-1707 (Oxford University Press, 2008).

Kilroy, Gerard, *Letter to TLS*, May 2, 2003, Times Online, http://tls.timesonline.co.uk
    Edmund Campion. Memory and Transcription, (Aldershot: Ashgate, 2005).

King Edward III, ed. Giorgio Melchiori (Cambridge: Cambridge Univ. Press, 1998).

Klause, John, "The Phoenix and Turtle in its Time," in Thomas Moisan and Douglas Bruster, ed., *In The Company of Shakespeare* (Fairleigh Dickinson Univ. Press, 2001).

"Politics, Heresy, and Martyrdom in Shakespeare's Sonnet 124 and Titus Andromicus," in James Schiffer, ed. *Shakespeare's Sonnets. Critical Essays* (New York: Garland Publishing, Inc. 1999).

Shakespeare, the Earl and the Jesuit (Cranberry, N.J.: Associated University Presses, 2008).

Knapp, Jeffrey, *Shakespeare's Tribe: Church Nation and Theatre in Renaissance England* (Chicago: Univ. of Chicago Press, 2002).

Lacey, Nicola, *A Life of H. L. A. Hart. The Nightmare And The Noble Dream* (Oxford: Oxford Univ. Press, 2004).

Langbein, John H., *Torture and the Law of Proof. Europe and England in the Ancien Régime* (Chicago: Univ. of Chicago Press, 1977).

Levin, Harry, *Shakespeare and the Revolution of the Times* (New York: Oxford Univ. Press, 1976).

Liber martyrorum, ed., Anon., Bodleian Library, Mss. Eng. Th. b.2.

Ligouri, Alfonso Maria de', *Theologia moralis*, ed. Leonard Gaudé (Graz, 1954 reprint of 1905 ed.).

Lutzenberger, Caroline, *The English Reformation And The Laity* (Cambridge: Cambridge Univ. Press, 1997).

Malone, Edmund, *Historical Account of the English Stage* (London, 1790).

Emendations and Additions (London 1790).

Marotti, Arthur F., *Religious Ideology and Cultural Fantasy. Catholic and Anti-Catholic Discourses In Early Modern England* (Notre Dame: Univ. of Notre Dame Press, 2005).

Martin, Patrick and Finnis, John, "Thomas Thorpe, 'W.S.' and the Catholic Intelligencers," *English Literary Renaissance* 33 (Winter, 2003).

Matchett, William H., *The Phoenix And The Turtle. Shakespeare's Poem And Chester's Love's Martyr* (The Hague: Mouton & Co. 1965).

Mateer, David, "William Byrd's Middlesex Recusancy," *Music and Letters* 78, 1-14 (1997).

Maus, Katharine Eisaman, "Introduction to Titus Adronicus," *The Norton Shakespeare*, ed. Stephen Greenblatt (New York: W.W. Norton &Company, 1997).

McClain, Lisa, *Lest We Be Damned. Practical Innovation And Lived Experience Among Catholics In Protestant England 1559-1642* (New York and London: Routledge, 2004).

McCoog, Thomas M., S.J., *The Society of Jesus In Ireland, Scotland, And England 1541-1588.* (Leiden: E.J. Brill 1996).

"Remembering Henry Garnet, S.J., " *Archivum Historicum Societatis Jesu,* January-June 2006.

"Playing the Champion," in McCoog, ed. *The Reckoned Expense: Edmund Campion And The Early English Jesuits* (Rome: Institutum Historicum Societatis Jesu, second ed., 2007).

McCoog and Peter Davidson, "Edmund Campion and William Shakespeare. Much Ado About Nothing?" in McCoog, *The Reckoned Expense, supra*, pp. 165-186.

McLaren, Angus, *Impotence. A cultural history* (Chicago: Univ. of Chicago Press, 2006).

McManaway, James G., "John Shakespeare's 'Spiritual Testament,'" *Shakespeare Quarterly* XVIII (1967) 197-205.

Melchiori, Giorgio. See *King Edward III*.

Michelangelo, *The Poetry of Michelangelo*, ed. James M. Saslaw (New Haven: Yale University Press, 1991).

Miller, Arthur, *Timebends. A Life* (New York: Grove Press, 1987).

Milward, Peter, S.J., *Shakespeare's Religious Background* (London: Sidgwick and Jackson, 1973).
   "Shakespeare's Passion Play," *The Renaissance Bulletin* 34:1 (2007).
   "Evidence Linking Shakespeare and the Jesuits," *Id.* 34:27 (2007).

Miola, Robert S., *Early Modern Catholicism. An Anthology of Primary Sources* (Oxford: Oxford Univ. Press, 2007).

Missale Romanum (New York: Benziger Brothers, 1956, reprint of the post-Tridentine missal).

Monson, Claude, "Bird, the Catholics and the Motet: The Hearing Reopened" in Dolores Pesce, ed. *Hearing The Motet. Essays on the Motet of the Middle Ages and Renaissance* (Oxford Univ. Press, 1997)

Murphy, Andrew, *Shakespeare in Print. A History And Chronology of Shakespeare Publishing* (Cambridge: Cambridge Univ. Press, 2003).

Mutshmann, Heinrich and Wentersdorf, Karl, *Shakespeare and Catholicism* (New York: Sheed and Ward, 1952).

The New Oxford Book of Carols, ed. Hugh Keyte and Andrew Parrott (Oxford: Oxford Univ. Press, 1992).

Nielson, William and Hill, Charles Jarvis, ed. *The Complete Plays and Poems of William Shakespeare* (Cambridge: Houghton Mifflin Company, 1941).

Noonan, John T. Jr., *A Church That Can And Cannot Change. The Development of Catholic Moral Teaching* (Norte Dame, Ind.: Univ. of Notre Dame Press, 2005).

"The Mermaid on the Dolphin's Back." *The Shakespeare News Letter* (Winter 2001/2002) No. 251.

Power to Dissolve. Lawyers and Marriages in the Courts of the Roman Curia (Cambridge, Mass. The Belknap Press of the Harvard Univ. Press, 1973).

Nuttall, A.D., *Shakespeare The Thinker* (New Haven: Yale Univ. Press, 2007).

O'Malley, John W., S.J. *The First Jesuits* (Cambridge: Harvard Univ. Press, 1993).

O'Neill, Eugene, *Long Day's Journey Into Night* (New Haven: Yale Univ. Press, 1989).

O.E.D. = *Oxford English Dictionary* (2nd ed., Oxford: Clarendon Press, 1989).

Parkinson, C. Northcote, *Gunpowder, Treason and Plot* (London: Weidenfeld and Nicholson, 1976).

Pilarz, Scott E., S.J., *Robert Southwell and the Mission of Literature 1561-1595* (Aldenshot: Ashgate Publishing Ltd., 2004).

Potter, Lois, "Having Our Will: Imagination In Recent Shakespeare Biographies," *Shakespeare Survey: Writing about Shakespeare*, ed. Peter Holland, vol. 58 (Cambridge: Cambridge Univ. Press, 2004).

Pregerson, Harry, Judge, opinion in *United States v Winters*, 729 F.2d 602, 605 (9th Cir. 1984).

Questier, Michael C., *Catholicism And Community In Early Modern England* (Cambridge: Cambridge Univ. Press, 2006).

Richmond, Velma Bourgeois, *Shakespeare Catholicism and Romance* (New York: Continuum, 2000).

Ripa, Cesare, *Iconologia* (New York, 1970, reprint of 1603 ed.).

Rollins, Hyder Edward, *The Phoenix Nest* (Cambridge: Harvard Univ. Press, 1930).

A New Variorum Edition of Shakespeare. The Poems (Philadelphia: J. B. Lippincott Co., 1938); *The Sonnets* (1943).

Rosenbaum, Ron, *The Shakespeare Wars* (New York: Random House, 2006).

Rubin, Miri, *Corpus Christi. The Eucharist in Late Medieval Culture* (Cambridge: Cambridge Univ. Press, 1991).

Rutherford, Richard, C.S.C., *Death of a Christian: The Rite of Funerals* (New York: Pueblo Publishing Co., 1980).

Sams, Eric, *The Real Shakespeare. Retrieving the Early Years, 1564-1594* (New Haven: Yale Univ. Press, 1994).
   Shakespeare's Edward III, ed. (New Haven: Yale Univ. Press, 1996).
Sanchez, Tomás, S.J., *In praecepta decalogi* (Lyons, 1643).

Sanudo, Marin, *Venice. Cità Excelentissina. Selections from the Renaissance Diaries of Marin Sanudo*, ed. Patrica Labalme and Laura Sangrinneti White. Translated by Linda L. Carroll. (Baltimore: The John Hopkins University Press, 2007).

Shakeen, Naseeb, *Biblical References in Shakespeare's Plays* (1999).

Shakespeare, William, *The Complete Works: The Norton Shakespeare*, ed. Stephen Greenblatt, et al. (New York: W. W. Norton &Company, 1997). This work based on the Oxford edition, contains all the plays and poems of Shakespeare. See also Booth, *supra*.

Shapiro, James, *A Year in the Life of William Shakespeare, 1599.* (New York: Harper Collins, 2005).

Shell, Alison, *Catholicism, Controversy And The English Literary Imagination* (Cambridge: Cambridge Univ. Press, 1999).

   Shakespeare and Religion (London: Arden 2010)

Shuger, Debora Kullen, *Political Theology In Shakespeare's England. The Sacred and the State in Measure for Measure* (New York: Palgrave, 2001).

Sir Thomas More, the play as presented by the Royal Shakespeare Comany (London, 2005; Nick Herm Books).

Southwell, Robert, S.J., *A Humble Supplication to Her Maiestie*, ed. R. C. Bald (Cambridge: at the Univ. Press, 1953).

   The Poems of Robert Southwell, S.J., ed. James D. McDonald and Nancy Pollard Brown (Oxford: at the Clarendon Press, 1967).

   St. Robert Southwell, Collected Poems, ed. Peter Davidson and Anne Sweeney (Manchester, Carcanet Press Ltd., 2007).

   Robert Southwell to his father, undated, Henry Foley, ed. *Records of the English Province of the Society of Jesus* (London: Burns & Oates, 1877) vol. I. First Series, 339-347.

   Spenser, Edmund, *The Faerie Queene* (London: Penguin Books, 1984).

The Splendor of Dresden (New York: Metropolitan Museum of Art, 1979).

Stevens, Wallace, "On Receiving The Gold Medal From The Poetry Society Of America," Stevens, *Opus Posthumous*, rev. and edited by Milton J. Bates (New York: Alfred A. Knopf, 1989).

Stubbs, John, *John Donne. The Reformed Soul* (New York: N.W. Norton & Co., 2006).

Sugg, Richard, *John Donne* (London: Palgrave Macmillan, 2007).

Swanson, R. N., *The Church and Mary* (Woodbridge, Suffolk: Boydell Press for the Ecclesiastical History Society, 2004).

Sweeney, Anne, *Robert Southwell. Snow in Arcadia* (Manchester: Manchester University Press, 2006).
Takcnaka, Masahiro, "Notes on John Shakespeare's Spiritual Testament," *The Renaissance Bulletin*, 34, 17 (2007).

Tanner, Norman P., S.J., *The Church in Late Medieval Norwich* (1370-1532), (Toronto: Pontifical Institute of Medieval Studies, 1984).

Taylor. Gary, "Forms of Opposition: Shakespeare and Middleton," *English Literary Renaissance* 24 (1994) 283-314.
   "The cultural politics of Maybe," in *Dutton, supra*, 242-258.
   "The date and auspices of the additions to *Sir Thomas More*" in T. H. Howard-Hill, *Shakespeare and Sir Thomas More: Essays on the Play and its Shakesperian Interest* (Cambridge: Cambridge University Press, 1989).

The Thirty-Nine Articles = A Theological Introduction to the Thirty-Nine Articles of the Church of England by E. J. Bicknell, third edition revised by H. J. Carpenter, bishop of Oxford (London: Longman, Green and Co., 1961).

Thomas a Kempis, *De imitatione Christi* (London: Kegan Paul, Trench, Trübner et soc., 1892).

Trimble, William Raleigh, *The Catholic Laity In Elizabethan England 1558-1603* (Cambridge: The Belknap Press of Harvard Univ. Press, 1964).

Tudor Church Music (Oxford: Oxford Univ. Press, 1st Series, 1928).

Vickers, Brian, *Counterfeiting Shakespeare* (Cambridge: Cambridge Univ. Press, 2002).
    Shakespeare Co-Author An Historical Study of Five Collaborative Plays (Oxford: Oxford University Press, 2002).

Warton, Thomas, *The History of English Poetry from the close of the eleventh to the commencement of the eighteenth century*, (London 1751, reprinted London 1998, Routledge/Thoemmes Press).

Weis, Rene, *Shakespeare Revealed. A Biography* (London: John Murray, 2007).

Wells, Stanley, *Shakespeare: Sex and Love* (Oxford: Oxford University Press, 2010).

Wigmore, John H., *Wigmore on Evidence*, ed. & rev. James Chadboun (Boston: Little, Brown and Co., 1978).

Williams, Glanville, *Criminal Law. The General Part* (London: Stevens & Sons 1961).

Wilson, Richard, *Secret Shakespeare. Studies in theatre, religion and resistance* (Manchester: Manchester Univ. Press, 2004).

Wizeman, William, Clergy & Staff at Corpus Christi Church: Sermons by Fr. Wizeman, www.corpus-christi-nyc.org/Sermons2. html.

Wood, Michael, *Shakespeare* (London, 2003).

Woodfield, Denis R., *Surreptitious Printing in England 1550-1640* (New York: Bibliographical Society of America, 1973).

Womersley, David, *Divinity and State* (Oxford: Oxford University Press, 2010).

Wymer, Rowland, "Shakespeare and the Mystery Cycle." *English Literary Renaissance* 24, 365 (2004).

Yeats, William Butler, "Three Movements," *The Collected Poems of W.B. Yeats* (New York: Scribner, 2nd Rev. Ed., 1996).

Zinman, Ira B., *Shakespeare's Sonnets And The Bible. A Spiritual Interpretation with Christian Sources*, (Bloomington, Ind.: World Windows, 2009).

CPSIA information can be obtained at www.ICGtesting.com
Printed in the USA
LVOW081535260612

287746LV00013B/44/P